Special Needs
in
Ordinary Classrooms

Blackwell Studies in Personal and Social Education and Pastoral Care

Edited by Peter Lang and Peter Ribbins

Leading a Pastoral Team
Les Bell and Peter Maher

Supportive Education
Phil Bell and Ron Best

School Discipline
Chris Watkins and Patsy Wagner

The Pastoral Curriculum
Lesley Bulman and David Jenkins

The Evaluation of Pastoral Care
Tony Clemett and John Pearce

Special Needs in Ordinary Classrooms

An Approach to Teacher Support and Pupil Care in Primary and Secondary Schools

Gerda Hanko

BASIL BLACKWELL

Published by Basil Blackwell Ltd
108 Cowley Road
Oxford OX4 1JF
England

British Library Cataloguing in Publication Data
Hanko, Gerda
  Special needs in ordinary classrooms: an approach
  to teacher support and pupil care in primary and
  secondary schools.
  1. Problem children——Education   2. Child
  psychotherapy
  I. Title
  371.94   LC4801

ISBN 0 631 14495 1
ISBN 0 631 14496 X Pbk

Typeset in 11/13pt Plantin Roman
by Katerprint Co. Ltd, Oxford.
Printed in Great Britain
by T. J. Press Ltd, Padstow, Cornwall

Contents

Acknowledgements
Introduction   1

Part I: Crossing Professional Boundaries

1 Bridging the gaps   9

2 Examples of case discussions with groups of teachers   13
   A teacher facing a sudden disturbing change in a child's
   behaviour   14
   Two examples of first case discussions   19
   How groups develop their expertise from case to case
   (i)   Development of skills in a three-term inter-school
          primary staff group   25
   (ii)   Development of skills in a two-term inter-school
          primary staff group   30
   (iii) Two case discussions of a two-term intra-school
          secondary staff group   36
   Preparing the ground for additional professional help   43

3 Staff support groups: an example of their development in one
   local area   48

Part II: A Framework for Teacher Support

4 Approaches to treatment and consultation   59
   Approaches to treatment   59
   The concept of consultation and its practice in schools   63

5 The meetings: purposes and foci   69
   Sharing knowledge   70

    (i) About the child   71

    (ii) About the classroom group   72

    (iii) About the teacher–pupil interaction   74

Restoring objectivity   76

Sharing skills   82

Restoring confidence   83

Special needs: the ordinary curriculum as a source of new
    learning experiences   85

Enlisting parents as partners   95

Part III: Providing Support: Guidelines and Tasks

6 Developing on-going support and training groups in a variety
of school settings: role and task of school-based or outside
consultants and of special needs co-ordinators   109

Knowing the obstacles   109

Initiating a teacher support group   112

    (i) First approaches within or to the institution   112

    (ii) Introducing consultancy support work to the teaching
        staff   116

Work with the groups   126

    (i) Early group meetings: fixed roles, hierarchies and
        expectations about the consultant's role   126

    (ii) Stages of development in the groups   129

    (iii) Case follow-ups   132

    (iv) Interpretations and interim evaluations   133

    (v) Endings and post-course follow-ups   137

Role and tasks of consultants and special needs co-ordinators   140

    (i) The special needs professional acting as school-based or
        outside consultant   140

    (ii) Role and tasks of the school-based special needs
        co-ordinator   145

7 Summary and conclusions: teacher support and pupil care in
the context of school-based in-service provision   148

Bibliography   154

*For simplicity alone (with no sexist implications) teachers and children
alike are referred to by the masculine pronoun.*

Acknowledgements

In the course of the work described in this book I have enjoyed meeting and being stimulated by a great number of people, all of whom I want to thank.

First of all, I am indebted to the late Irene Caspari for introducing me, over two decades ago, to the possibilities of consultation as a mode of working with teachers and student-teachers in the classroom context and to Ben Morris, Professor Emeritus, Bristol School of Education, and Evelyn Carter, lately Principal of Thomas Huxley College, Ealing, for their long-standing interest in my pursuit of this approach to teacher support and training, and encouragement in my writing about it.

I also want to express particular thanks to the following: to Pat Southgate, co-ordinator of the DES-funded Schools and In-Service Teacher Education (SITE) Evaluation Project (Ealing) 1978–1980, for the opportunity of having the approach evaluated within the project; to Reginald Hartles, Chief Education Officer, Ealing, and Joyce Shepherd, until recently Chief Education Inspector, for supporting further evaluation and development of the approach in the schools of their borough in association with the University of London Institute of Education; to Tony Cline, Principal Educational Psychologist, ILEA, and John Cooper, Director of Education, Hounslow, for affording me facilities to explore the approach further in different settings and areas; to the staffs of child guidance clinics, centres and organisations who invited me to talk to them, for the invaluable exchange of ideas and of experience that this entailed; above all to the teachers and headteachers of schools whose active and evaluative participation in the groups constantly offered me fresh indications of the kind of support that they could use and helped me to attempt to develop practice and principles for charting this area of in-service work.

My very special thanks are due to Molly Brearley, Elizabeth Irvine and Dr. Mary Wilson who kindly read the typescript and commented on it most helpfully. Elizabeth Irvine also helped me in the earlier drafts of the script to deal with the many vicissitudes of first-language interference in my writing. Having my own special educational needs attended to at this stage of my professional career, I am able to acknowledge first hand those who stress that all children have special needs and that the special needs concept should not entail categorisation. Where the concept appears in the text, it is used with this understanding of all children's needs being special, but of some children needing extra attention at some stage during their life at school, to promote fullest possible participation in an educational enterprise worth their while.

Introduction

A 7-year-old attends a new school, hates everybody and is in trouble every day. A 9-year-old's behaviour changes 'out of the blue' from an ideal pupil to an unmanageable trouble-maker. Fifth-form Teresa's provocative rule-breaking gets worse the more she is reprimanded for it, and 15-year-old John's does not improve even when his teachers bend over backwards to give him another chance. When asked to stop it, he dares his teachers to hit him and threatens to thump them if they do. 6-year-old Michael panics at everything that he is asked to do for himself; so does 8-year-old Don but, when Don is helped to improve, Martin takes over. Nothing can get Ivan (10 years old), out of his shell. Dave (8 years old), is 'an infuriating boy who never listens and can't even copy from the board'. 9-year-old Jeanie's 'fussy, attention-seeking helpfulness' is so irritating that no one wants to work or play with her; and Dipak (14 years old), waylays staff at every corner with requests. His teachers have tried to help but 'lost all sympathy' when he started lying to them.

The twin themes of this book are the many children in need of extra attention for emotional, behavioural and related learning problems in mainstream classrooms and the support that is owed to their teachers. Teachers are faced with the task to respond instantaneously to situations such as the above, but are also confronted with numerous obstacles to doing so appropriately. They cannot be expected to meet such children's needs if they get no support with their own.

Teachers may find exceptional behaviour disturbing to varying degrees and may respond to it in a number of ways without fully understanding what special needs it expresses. They may see a problem as located in the child, in his family and home or in the child's situation at school, in conflict with what is expected of him.

They may not recognise those special needs which do not lead to behaviour problems, and consequently these may remain unmet and worsen. There are also general behaviour problems, not themselves expressive of special needs but related to those of individual children, which teachers need to deal with in order to benefit the personal development and educational progress of both the individual child and the other children.

This book is concerned with such dimensions of need where teachers find themselves least supported. It has been written in response to growing demands from three main directions.

1 Teachers across the whole range of mainstream schools feel that they need support for their work with pupils — seen as disturbed and disturbing — whose special emotional and resulting educational needs they fear they are failing to meet.

2 There is dissatisfaction among those specially qualified to alleviate the emotional needs of individual children. They are conscious that they are able to assist only a very small number of children when many need help and that they provide this assistance away from the classroom, where the problems occur.

3 There is now official acceptance of the need for improvement in the education service through the professional development of teachers, including: the necessity for all teachers to be able to respond appropriately to the exceptional needs they encounter (as advocated by the Advisory Committee on the Supply and Education of Teachers (ACSET, 1984)); concern as to how this is best facilitated through teacher education at all levels (which the committee for Research into Teacher Education (CRITE) state in their objectives); growing interest in school-based and school-focused in-service work shown in national research projects supported by the Department of Education and Science (DES) such as the Schools and In-Service Teacher Education (SITE) Evaluation Project (Baker and Sikora, 1982)) and Schools Council programmes such as Guidelines for Review and Internal Development in Schools (GRIDS) (McMahon *et al*, 1984)).

The documents cited above have increased awareness of what is involved in *Making INSET work* (DES, 1978) and manifest a growing understanding of a number of issues. It is these issues which are addressed in the approach to teacher support described in this book. They are concerned with what is involved in professional development and what obstacles militate against this, the difficulties that teachers experience in identifying their professional needs or in using the provision offered to meet them, the difficulties that providers have in gearing their provision to the context in which teachers work, to be of both *immediate* and *long-term* use in the classroom and school setting, and how to offer this in such a way that it is usable and acceptable while maintaining teachers' autonomy.

Such provision rules out prescriptive advice and intrusive exhortations on what a school or a teacher should do. It recognises, appreciates and builds on teachers' existing strengths and expertise. Ultimately, it creates conditions favourable to finding workable solutions and produces a climate of commitment and mutual respect in which the teachers themselves, as individuals and as a team, can implement their conclusions and observe and consider what needs evolve.

This book introduces teachers in ordinary schools to the potential of special needs related school-based staff support and training groups which many teachers and headteachers already find valuable. It also looks at the possibilities, principles and practicalities of developing such groups by those able to initiate them. These may be the school's own special needs support or pastoral teachers and counsellors, or they may come from outside, such as members of child guidance, school psychological and social services, teaching hospitals, tutorial units, local advisers responsible for in-service support and training, teachers in special schools willing to collaborate with their mainstream colleagues, or tutors of professional training courses. All these would be capable of sharing some of their skills and understanding in a way that can be applied within the teacher's educational remit.

While it has been stressed that all children's educational needs are special and require individual responses in the educational process, varying figures are given of children who need special assistance in school lest the severity of their needs should impair the quality of their education. These figures depend on the criteria used to define and identify such special needs, on what we define as special support and on whom we envisage in the role of supporter. Warnock (1978) gives an overall figure of 20%, composed of 2% now educated in special schools and 18% in ordinary schools who are likely to need special help at some time. Kolvin *et al* (1982) identified 25% of children between seven and eight years old as needing treatment for behavioural, emotional and relationship difficulties. Daines *et al* (1981) ascertained nearly 30% of third-year children in four comprehensive schools as having relatively severe problems. These figures give weight to the Advisory Committee's advocacy (ACSET, 1984) that provision should be made to enable *all* teachers to become responsive to children's special needs. It is clear that neither internal pastoral care

3

and special needs support teachers nor external specialists can possibly meet the needs of such a number of children by dealing personally with one case after another. They can, however, hope to meet the need by augmenting the ability of teachers to help such children and, in the process, many others. As Kolvin *et al* (1982) stress, teachers need both professional and emotional support in this area; they need to be helped, 'interactionally' to adapt their approach to these children's individual needs if educational gains are to accompany any success in the relief of their emotional problems.

Without such support the difficulties for teachers and some pupils can seem insurmountable. Teachers often feel ill-equipped to respond to this range of emotional and behaviour difficulties of 'disturbed' children, although many of these may be only slightly more severe than similar problems experienced by the many 'normal' children who manage to cope with them without displaying 'abnormal' behaviour. Moreover, such difficulties can provoke reactions in teachers which increase rather than reduce the problems. Many teachers battle on without the professional and emotional support which they could receive from those with special expertise, such as their own pastoral, counselling and special needs coordinators or outside specialists.

Research evidence confirms (Schools Council, 1968; Raven, 1977–8) that teachers are deeply concerned with their pupils as people. They may feel committed to develop the interests and to respond to the needs of all their pupils but may at the same time feel unable to do so in many cases which they find baffling and stressful. The children whom they are trying to help may seem to obstruct their efforts and to make them feel useless. Teachers may blame the children and their background for this, or they may feel that pressures in the school system are interfering with their ability to respond adequately to such children's needs. Either way, they may feel that they have to handle the difficulties predominantly in terms of control and that they can give little help to the pupil. As Medway (1976) convincingly described, they may feel compelled to resort to merely 'coping', which they may themselves despise but which allows them to keep going, albeit at a reduced level of functioning and a high level of stress. They may fall back on defensive encounters with disaffected children, whose needs become ever less likely to be met. Thus, children with special emotional, behaviour and learning needs and behaviour difficulties, whom teachers could in fact help within their educational remit and the normal constraints of the system, tend not to receive the early help to which they would in all probability have been able to respond. Such children may then continue to indicate their needs in ways which educational institutions must find unacceptable, thereby worsening their difficulties.

Teachers are also often hindered by some unhelpful beliefs and myths in their profession regarding 'special needs' children: that children deemed to be maladjusted are of a different kind and differ qualitatively from 'normal' children; that teachers' professional skills are inherently and unavoidably insufficient for dealing with them (despite evidence to the contrary (cf. Rutter *et al* (1979) and Rutter (1985) who cite evidence that good experiences at school can at least partially compensate for difficulties at home); that salvation can come from special needs experts (to whom one may therefore send the children if they are within the school, or to whom, if they are external, one may resort only in desperation and when the stigma can no longer be avoided).

The specialists' skills, however, and the principles and practices with which they relieve emotional problems are as yet only rarely conveyed to teachers. These specialists increasingly agree that children and teachers may be spared much distress and that much waste of emotional energy and educational potential can be prevented, if some of the knowledge and skill is made available to teachers in general. A growing number of these professionals, from the range of institutions listed on p. 3, now attempt to help teachers to respond better to their pupils' special needs, deepening the teachers' understanding, and optimising and maximising their educational skills and resources.

Joining their expertise across the traditional boundaries of apparently conflicting professional orientations and expectations, such professionals can base their approach on principles formulated by pioneers of group consultation such as Balint (1957), Caplan (1970) and Kadushin (1977), and now have the benefit of individual workers' accounts (cf. Skynner, 1974; Irvine, 1979; Dowling and Osborne, 1985) of their adaptation to a school setting. Working with groups of teachers as consultants, they interpret their role in various ways, and mostly exercise it unsupported in an uncharted field. Many specialists are therefore diffident about tackling the obstacles involved in crossing these boundaries and about dealing with the tensions and anxieties in a work setting whose effectiveness largely depends on the extent to which these are resolved. Research reviews (Conoley, 1981) suggest, however, that teachers welcome any viable support which is offered in this field.

I have tried to put into this book what I have learnt about the needs of children and teachers in over three decades of working with them. Evaluations elsewhere of the approach described here (Baker and

Sikora, 1982; Hanko, 1982; Hider, 1981) permit us to focus on the issues facing 'in-house' and external consultants to teachers. How aware are teachers of the perceptions which children with special needs, their parents and the teachers themselves have of each other, and of the effect that these can have on work in the classroom? How much knowledge of emotional and behaviour difficulties can be of help to teachers in ordinary schools and therefore ought to be made available to them? How can they, often overworked and under stress as they are, best acquire such insight and information so that it is of immediate and long-term use to them and to the children? What skills do those who offer support to teachers need themselves, to be able to extend those of their teaching colleagues?

I shall examine in Part I the divide which exists between teachers and those with additional psychological expertise, both inside and outside schools, and how it may be bridged to lead to an on-going consultative support and training service which reaches a maximum number of teachers. I shall then give examples of case discussions in a range of school-based settings to show how classroom teachers and headteachers have made use of and consolidated the bridge and have themselves helped to further the service in their local area.

In Part II, I shall discuss the framework of such staff consultation in relation to the different theoretical bases and practices employed by the various experts in the field, comparing psychodynamic and behavioural consultancy with regard to problem assessment, choice and implementation of treatment. There follows an analysis of objectives and of how these may be achieved in relation to both child and teacher in their particular work settings. This includes special sections on how teachers can be helped to make optimal use of the ordinary curriculum as a source of learning experiences to help to meet special needs, and how they can enlist parents as partners in their endeavours.

Part III offers some guidelines for initiating and developing support and training groups in a variety of school settings. It deals with the role and tasks of external and internal staff consultants and special needs coordinators, the skills required of them in their work with fellow professionals and how these may influence the development of an on-going support system. I conclude by summarising the possibilities of consultancy support to maximise existing resources in the context of school-based in-service development.

PART I
Crossing Professional Boundaries

1
Bridging the Gaps

Those who are already working with teachers in ordinary schools, either as special needs pastoral specialists on the school staff or as consultants from the outside support services, confirm that teachers are troubled by the discrepancy between their actual response to many special needs and that required, that they therefore respond to a form of in-service support and training which succeeds in offering them knowledge and skill to reduce this gap, that such support can tap and maximise more resources than teachers are often given credit for, and enables them to use their insight and skills to work with and to help those pupils who give them special concern. There are, however, a number of obstacles which can prevent such support from developing. Those aiming to offer it therefore need to take account of the psychological and institutional difficulties which may militate against its acceptance or implementation, so that these may be resolved.

The possibilities for redeploying the skills of psychologically qualified professionals from the guidance and welfare network outside the schools and pastoral/remedial/special needs support systems within them have been elaborated in a number of accounts[1] since its early advocacy in official reports (Summerfield, 1968) and circulars (DES/DHSS, 1974). Leading experts (Tizard, 1973; Wall, 1973) and practitioners (cf. Caspari, 1976; Cline, 1980) have urged them for more than a decade not to confine their attention to the few cases referred to them but to address themselves to the problems of *teachers* in ordinary classrooms which contain so many children in need of extra attention. At the same time, they reminded both teachers and special needs experts that teachers are the only professionals in daily contact with all school-age children and have a unique opportunity to offer them new learning experiences which could help to meet their special needs. It was also emphasised that many opportunities remain unused if teachers do not get qualified support to deepen their insights into such needs and to extend their skills and resources to apply them.

In spite of growing dissatisfaction, both in the schools and in the special support services, with such waste of existing expertise (Galloway and Goodwin, 1979; Gillham, 1978), recent evidence (Hegarty and Pocklington, 1981) suggests that most teachers still perceive the experts as inaccessible — in spite of these experts' offer of an apparently 'open door' — except for occasional communication on the exceptionally severe cases which they have referred. There are many teachers who expect that the experts will not involve them or who view their skills as inapplicable to ordinary classrooms. Neither side seems to find it easy to change the status quo. The teachers do not know how best to invite those with special expertise to share it with them, and those who have the experience have doubts about how to offer it to their colleagues in the classrooms. As a result, both specialist services and the schools that they serve remain needlessly enmeshed in what have been called 'tip-and-run' arrangements (Mittler, 1985) and unnecessarily inadequate in each other's eyes. When schools turn to the specialist services as a last resort, they clearly are not asking them for professional support when the special needs first show themselves, at the time when the special needs might be met by the teacher with support, before they become less tractable. Teachers who use the services only when convinced that the child is impossible to cope with may thereby imply that the problem resides in the child and, as Galloway (1985) argues, transfer responsibility to the specialist, thus absolving themselves from considering their inter- action with the child or from looking for the precipitating factors in a crisis. Help is traditionally offered away from the situation in which the difficulty occurs and reaches only the referred child. It does not reach those with whom he interacts in the classroom, nor the many other children who could benefit from the kind of understanding offered to him. Children referred at the point of crisis are apt to experience referral as renewed abandonment by the teacher, which may or may not be the opposite of what was intended but which certainly adds to the difficulty of treatment. Lastly, referral may suggest to parents that they have failed or may trigger off other fears they dare not face. They may then withhold co-operation or, if coaxed into accepting an appointment, may not keep it — children then becoming 'referred-but-not-seens' (Mearns' and Kay's (1985) RBNSs) — or may fail to return, thus leaving the teacher to cope without support until the child transfers his difficulties to the next school.

Traditional referral arrangements nourish the beliefs and myths of maladjustment as a distinct condition, salvation by experts, and ordinary teaching skills and resources as insufficient or unrelated to cases of special need. These perpetuate the sharp division between special expertise and ordinary teaching and can foster defensiveness between professionals who should be working as partners.

Teachers complain that they cannot obtain the kind of information which might help them to be more supportive to the child which they have referred; they deride the experts, who 'only tell us what we already knew', or ignore their written advice as impractical if they lack opportunities to discuss the issues with them. Perfunctory entries in school records that 'Tom has been seen by the psychologist' further suggest that the content or conclusions of the session were not deemed to be his teachers' business or within their competence.

Those with special expertise, however, may notice only the teachers' inadequate handling of the child prior to referral and may show concern that teachers seem to use them as a dumping ground. They may fail to appreciate how the demands of the school system can blunt teachers' sensitivity to children's emotional difficulties and to under-estimate the obstacles (including the stress that teachers may be undergoing when working with difficult children in front of a class) which interfere with an appropriate response to them. The specialists' advice may then imply criticism of the teacher and appear irrelevant to the classroom. Both sides frequently feel unappreciated and unfavourably judged by the other. This can make teachers doubtful about offers of support by 'omniscient' experts and increases the obstacles for experts trying to reconstruct their service, to redeploy their skills and to include in their remit systematic, rather than incidental, support work to reach a maximum number of teachers.

Yet there are accounts which show that groups of teachers and those with special expertise in the field of exceptional emotional and educational needs can work together. This is in spite of a widespread view that 'getting teachers to work together is a problem' (Eavis, 1983) and that 'professional pride is a major barrier to teachers sharing their anxieties and frustrations in attempts to tackle their difficulties' (Spencer, 1983). Although such apprehensions are not unfounded, teachers are the first to refute them, once a way has been found to establish such groups. They are eager to deepen their understanding of pupils' emotional and behavioural difficulties as part of their professional task and *educational* concern, as their own latent skills and resources are released. These resources may have remained un-tapped owing to mistaken beliefs about the separateness of educational and welfare functions and the extent to which teachers can make a difference to children's special needs. Teachers may have been insufficiently aware of the significance of their observations and knowledge about a child's situation to be able to identify the special needs underlying the observed behaviour and to adapt their teaching to them. Alternatively, they may have based even considered opinions on inadequate knowledge and understanding or on partial or distorted perceptions.

I shall first try to show, for the benefit of teachers hesitant about requesting support, how school-based support and training groups can deal with issues such as these, to encourage them to invite their own special needs support or pastoral colleagues to examine these issues with them. In the later sections, I shall discuss the role of special needs consultant and support staff, whether on the school's staff or external, and examine the preliminaries necessary for establishing staff support groups and the skills required for their development.

Note

1 See, for instance:

Caspari (1962), Skynner (1974), Wall (1977; 1979), Gillham (1978), Daines *et al* (1981) and Dowling and Osborne (1985) (on the case for child guidance and schools psychological services staff); Lyons (1973) and Irvine (1979) (from the social work perspective); Wilson and Evans (1980), Garrett (1983) and Mittler (1984) (for special schools staff); Barrett (1985), Clunies-Ross (1984), Lewis (1984), Sewell (1982), Smith (1982) and NARE (1979; 1982) (for remedial teachers); Dunkley (1980), Fuller (1982), Fulton (1980), Longley (1980) and Sisterton (1980) (for the case of counsellors); Blackburn (1983), Bulman (1984), Button (1983), Taylor (1984), Mayes (1985), Ribbins (1985) and Stagles (1985) (for pastoral care, tutorial and middle management staff).

2
Examples of Case Discussions with Groups of Teachers

I shall try to show how the teachers who participated in these discussions increasingly felt that they managed to handle more appropriately the difficulties that they had with some of their pupils, none of whom I had met. This happened because they were learning how to widen their perception of the problems so that they could be translated into interaction terms, on the basis that the disturbance-producing situations and backgrounds were better understood. By taking into account the child's likely experience of both the situation and its antecedents, using quite precise questions about the child and the classroom context, the teachers were helped to see for themselves how aspects of a child's situation might have created the difficulties or might be maintaining them; the teachers discovered how they might, by educational means, improve the situation and those of other children with similar problems.

The children discussed are selected partly because of the range of problems described by their teachers, partly to demonstrate how work in the groups developed in a range of primary and secondary school settings, at different stages in the life of a group, and partly to show how the situations discussed and the solutions attempted are of equal relevance to primary and secondary schools (some groups contained teachers from both).

The discussions are described in sufficient detail to show the step-by-step development of issues as they suggested to the teachers workable solutions, both for the child under consideration and as part of the problem-solving framework that developed in consecutive sessions. As will be seen, no attempt was made to categorise the children, who could have been variously labelled as emotionally disturbed, socially disturbing, troubled or troublesome, gifted but difficult, or slow-learning, with a range of symptoms, nor was there any attempt to classify their behaviour, to offer clinical diagnoses or to suggest a modified form of clinical treatment. In other words, no decisions were made for the teachers, and they were not encouraged to perceive the children solely in terms of their difficulties. Instead, we focused on the context of the concern and the disturbance; on the children's differing reactions, on what these seemed to indicate about their expectations of others and their view of themselves, on the past experiences which can produce such expectations and on the new learning experiences which might favourably amend expectations and extend the children's view of themselves and of others relating to them.

All names are fictitious, and identifying detail has been omitted.

A teacher facing a sudden disturbing change in a child's behaviour

Teachers in any kind of school may suddenly be confronted with a child in turmoil and may be unsure how to react. It certainly worried Mrs. A. when she faced the changes in Tony.

Tony
'Something terrible is happening in my class with Tony; can we — please! — talk about him today?' was the first remark in the group session. As in other schools in this multiproblem city area, the staff of Tony's school (a junior school) and of the adjacent infant school were meeting weekly to discuss, with me as an outside consultant, how best to work with those children whose behaviour caused them concern. This was their fourth meeting, and they had intended to explore another child's case, but their colleague implored them to make time for Tony. In view of this urgency they agreed to try and discuss two cases in this session, giving about 45 minutes to each.

Mrs. A. briefly told the group that 9-year-old Tony had been a sound learner, most helpful with other children and a splendid member of the class. She had always found it easy to have a good relationship with him. She knew that he and his older brother were brought up by his father and paternal grandparents, who seemed to be out of touch with his mother. The school had heard that his mother had been imprisoned many years previously and was full of admiration for the father and grandparents for the caring home that they provided and the very active, busy life that they led which gave the boys plenty of stimulation through many events and entertainments.

In the previous week, however, during the class's news period, the children's talk had turned from a news item on 'Thieves Caught Red-handed' to the question of whether such people should or should not be sent to prison. Tony had then suddenly got up, told the class that his Mum had been sent to prison many years ago, and that he did not know whether she was still there or whether she was dead. He then sat down, white and silent for the rest of the afternoon, but from the next day had turned into a 'demon' in class and playground, constantly interfering with other children. He was now an unmanageable trouble-maker, after having previously been 'mature for his age'. The teacher, disturbed at this transformation, told the group how she had been trying to cope by keeping the whole class as busy as she could so that there would be no chance for anybody to mention what Tony had told them. As she was saying this, however, she interrupted herself, suddenly wondering whether her own frantic busy-ness was perhaps similar to what was happening at Tony's home all the time, with everybody trying to keep the children's minds occupied with other matters in order to 'protect' the children. She wondered what was the right thing to do? Should she just go on trying to manage Tony somehow, hoping that it would all eventually die down? What was Tony wanting her to do?

In the discussion which followed, the group was guided to focus on the stress felt separately by the child *and* by the teacher. Was it possible to share the stress *with* the child? He had, after all, been close to his teacher beforehand. Had the event not been a communication of something which nobody seemed able to share with him but which was bound to dominate his thoughts? Had his outburst also led to the loss of a necessary barrier, which he now did not know how to do without and perhaps needed to restore? Were his feelings and anxieties now complicated and intensified by having given away the 'family secret' to the whole world? Was there any way in which the teacher could show that she understood all this, without intruding any further, and in which the child could be left to make use of the teacher's understanding? Would it perhaps be possible, eventually, also to convey to the father how important it was for children to be allowed to talk about a missing parent and to think well of her?

Mrs. A. was left with these questions in mind, and the group turned to their second case. She had found the discussion helpful and was relieved that others had been able to share her anxieties about Tony. A fortnight later she reported that, 2 days after the discussion, she had managed to find a good moment, after 'another awful day with Tony', to have a quiet talk with him. She had told him that she had noticed how differently he had been behaving lately, how difficult all this was for everybody, how it had all started after he had told them about his Mum and how worried he probably was about it all. She had said that she understood what he must be feeling, and that if he wanted to talk to her about it, she would always have time for him but that if he did not want to, that would be alright, too. Since then, his troublesome behaviour had ceased. He had not accepted her invitation to talk but was again relating well to her and to the other children.

We could have left it at that, had the purpose of the group been merely to give teachers an opportunity to get together to share their problems about dealing with specific cases. However, more is required if such case-focused analysis is to aid a training process in which insights gained about a specific case can be conceptualised to become part of a framework for dealing with similar problems as they arise. Such conceptualisation was attempted in this group by inviting the teachers to examine in depth Tony's disturbing behaviour and its termination.

It was suggested to the group that the cessation of the boy's troublesome behaviour, and his more relaxed way of relating to others afterwards, seemed to show that he felt understood and that he had needed his feelings to be acknowledged. It seemed that the teacher had managed to help him to 'reach back over the gap of his breakdown and forward to renewed good relationships', as has been described in other similar cases (Winnicott, 1965). Intuitively, the teacher had understood his aggressive behaviour as a sign of panic, and his interference with the work of other children — stopping them from functioning — as a message of distress. She was helped to see both as representations of 'traumatic — unthinkable — experience at an early age' (Dockar-Drysdale, 1973), triggered off by the stimulus of the news period on prisons. She had also realised, as she presented the case, how sheltering children from talking about troubling events such as the loss of a parent, as both she and Tony's family had tried to do, may have more to do with the adults' own needs than with those of the children.

This intuitive understanding of the incident and its causes had been shared in the consultation and been thought through in detail, which led to tentative but systematic reformulation of the problem. The earlier build-up of an apparently mature 'false self' and its breakdown were noted, together with the hope of being understood which was shown by acting out the 'unthinkable anxiety' in anti-social behaviour. The teacher's tentative verbalisation of the child's feelings had been a sign to him of her attempt to understand his 'own version of his existence' (Winnicott, 1965); she had shown her ability to accept his unthinkable anxiety, and to make it thinkable by sharing it, while setting limits to his acting out his feelings in anti-social ways. She had also shown willingness to help him to face these feelings by expressing them in a safe relationship, but only if he wanted to do so. His message was received and accepted, his despair and his hope had been noted, and it was left to him to decide whether to engage in further communication or to rebuild whatever barrier he needed. She had facilitated the 'spontaneous processes of self-repair' (Winnicott, 1965)), while stopping short of an interpretive approach, which lies beyond the range or scope of the teacher.

In the group discussions the teachers experienced what Bion (1970) described as 'liberation into conceptualisation', when intuition (the teacher's) is shared and further knowledge applied to each detail, facilitating the search for workable solutions. Tony's case helped the teachers to realize how the apparent maturity of a child's false self can induce us to accept the surface for the whole person, leaving us at a loss to understand 'unintelligible' behaviour changes. The example also suggested that to react to surface behaviour symptoms by attempting to make them disappear without understanding what need they expressed would have been likely to increase the underlying need, even if the symptoms could have been suppressed.

In Tony's case, one could also point out that more was probably being achieved than a desirable short-term result, as has been suggested by others (Wolff, 1969; Rutter, 1981) and that — apart from helping the child to contain an acutely poignant experience — such on-the-spot yet unobtrusive help during a crisis uses a time of particular receptivity to help and further understanding. This may also strengthen the child's coping capacities for the future, since he experiences — as did the teachers in the group — that one can 'deal with one's life problems by one's own efforts and with the help of others — and a repertoire of learned skills for solving them' (Caplan, 1982). The teachers gained in skill through learning that one can help disturbed children to understand and to express their feelings (or, as in this case, to hear them expressed), so that they themselves change their behaviour as a result of understanding themselves better.

Lastly, the group was asked to turn their thoughts to the father. Could more be done for Tony and his brother, if he could be helped to understand that Tony, like other children who live with only one parent, may need to talk about his absent mother, to understand and think well of her and to gain some access to the reality of her existence and that this will help him to cope with otherwise 'unthinkable' anxieties and fantasies? As clinical evidence shows (Bowlby, 1979), support like this can make a great difference to both lone parent and child. We took into account how distressed the father would be, if he had heard about the incident, at having the family secret spread all over the school through Tony's outburst. However, there was also evidence of the strength with which he cared for his sons. It was again left to Mrs. A.'s discretion to see whether it was possible to involve the father without thereby adding to Tony's problems.

Summary

To sum up, Mrs. A. had started the session with a question of how best to help a child's crisis behaviour which was sparked off by ordinary everyday classroom activity. The discussions in the group made a difference to Tony and to Mrs. A. who had herself become anxious about his behaviour change. She, too, had found that her anxieties could be shared and carried professionally, her strengths could be recognised, her concerns accepted and her reactions put into objective perspective. Understanding was deepened in the whole group as issues were highlighted in joint exploration, so that suggestions for appropriate action arose from the teachers' own growing insight, instead of being imposed from outside. The teacher's decision was part of her expertise and clarification. She had seen Tony's disturbing behaviour as an invitation to act, which she then managed to do in her own effectively tentative way.

Having to solve problems like these can be a burden for teachers who have rarely learned during training not only to be aware of how children's family situations may adversely affect their progress at school but also to use such understanding in their relations with the children and in sensitive parent–teacher partnerships to enhance the children's progress. Mrs. A., like her colleagues, had found their joint analysis of these issues thought provoking, and considerations like these became a feature of their later case discussions, as we shall see when we rejoin them in their concern for Dave and Jeanie below. First we turn to two very different groups and their earliest case explorations.

Two examples of first case discussions

The nature and extent of the difficulty which groups present in their first cases, will be influenced by the way that support has been initiated and membership has been recruited, and by how hopeful or dubious they are about its value.

Teresa

Teresa's case was presented in a group of secondary school teachers, all of whom were heads of houses or year tutors. The group was organised by the deputy head, who had heard of such groups working well in other schools of the area. At the first meeting, Teresa was described as an 'anti-authority problem', aggravated by the school's well-intentioned efforts to enlist the father's help, which had misfired because he always disciplined her severely for any misdemeanour.

Teresa's housemaster told us that she had been reported by several masters for breaking school rules just to get attention; she was a bright girl, but never completed her work with them. She was now in the fifth form. She lived with her father, an ageing grandmother (who had both come from India in their adult years), an older brother and a younger sister. All three children attended the same school. The mother had left the family many years ago and now had a new family. Teresa visited her occasionally, but less and less often, as she felt that she was in the way.

Her rule-breaking mainly consisted in slipping out of school during school hours, blatantly in full sight of the master on duty. When challenged, she would refuse to give any explanation; 'like a wall' when reprimanded, she seemed to dare teachers to reprimand her by this open breaking of rules. The more she was reprimanded, the worse she became. When asked to help the school in this matter, the father had insisted that each new incident should at once be reported to him. He would then cane her for it. The teachers had therefore not contacted him again, and he then instructed his son to report on her. He seemed to follow these instructions diligently.

When the group explored the whole situation, they noticed that Teresa openly defied only men teachers, whom she seemed to manipulate into rejecting and restricting her like her father. The woman teacher in the group, who also taught her, spoke well of her and had been unaware of these difficulties. She had found her quiet in class, always complying, albeit minimally so, and never volunteering to answer any questions. She looked extremely unhappy at times. This teacher then also mentioned that the younger sister, who had just joined the school, was beginning to behave oddly and becoming very attention seeking.

Encouraged to think about the situation of this adolescent girl, so blatantly rejected by the male members of her family and with no mother to turn to, the teachers agreed that it would be a good idea to give her the opportunity of feeling that men could be on her side. They felt that it might help if the men teachers tried not to be stage managed into acting as reprimanding guards and to be as accepting and helpful as possible, without expecting an immediate positive response, however. They discussed whether they might not renew their contact with the father more constructively and might persuade him to accept his daughters better and perhaps to discuss with him how severe punishment often made behaviour worse, how none of us likes to be threatened and how we all tend to work more happily when we feel accepted. They also explored how they might help Teresa to cope with her situation, thought of elements in the curriculum which could give pupils in general a deeper understanding of how human beings relate and what difficulties they can experience, in societies all over the world, within and between generations, and of the different ways that people find to deal with them.

At a follow-up meeting two terms after the end of this group's one-term course, Teresa's case came up as one of the happiest developments: She had planned to leave both school and home at the end of her fifth year but, unable to find a job, had returned the following autumn. She had begun to confide in one of the men teachers who had been trying to relate to her along the lines that we had discussed and had told him what a shock it had been to her to see how upset her father had been to learn of her unhappiness and her wish to leave the family home. The teacher had then tried to help her to understand her father's probable feelings, had talked about what loss and separation do to people and had since then noticed in Teresa a striking depth of understanding. She had told him later that 'things are better now at home'. He had also noticed that she was now being met by a boy-friend at the school gates at the end of the day. There had been no recurrence of her challenging behaviour this year.

Although this had been a group's first case discussion, the teachers, in contrast with their earlier reprimanding treatment, had found a way of providing at least some support in this girl's stifled struggle for independence and, judging by what she said and how she changed, had perhaps also helped her to begin to develop the kind of under-standing which may enable her to cope with her childhood scars.

They had considered the restrictive role that she had 'made' them play and had examined how they might develop their relationship with a 'hopeless' parent who seemed to be endangering a pupil's progress, in addition to what helpful learning experiences they might provide for the whole class through skilful use of the *curriculum*. Remaining cautious about further contact with her father, they had nevertheless been able to help Teresa through acceptance, support and respect for her dignity, to change her reactions to her father's treatment sufficiently for her both to assert herself and to feel for him and also to secure for herself an improvement at home and better relations outside. No doubt she would have found such support even more helpful if relations at home had not improved.

The teachers whom she had so blatantly provoked into dealing with her severely had been enabled to see her aggressive provocations in a different light, had ceased to be provoked, had begun to support her struggling maturity and had helped her to face what was threatening her maturing self. They did so by demonstrating to her that attitude of concern for others through which one can accept 'good' and 'bad' as parts of a whole person and can understand better the needs of those who did not appear to show the same concern. She could do this as her own problems were understood and she was helped to cope with them. It seems to pay dividends on several accounts if teachers take time to listen to their pupils, and to each other's experience of them. Teresa's teachers shared their differing experiences of her in a consultative back-up setting in which her responses in different situations and to different teachers — apparently contradictory — took on a new meaning which enabled the teachers to see her in a different light and to help her. This ameliorated her situation both at school and at home, beneficially affected the relationship between child and parent and drew attention to the possible problems of siblings, whose 'oddities' (the sister's symptoms and the brother's uncharitable behaviour) had until then been noted but not been attended to.

It would be naive to think that the difficulties of all pupils from ethnic minorities, straddling such disparate cultural and inter-generational problems, can be similarly resolved, but problems such as Teresa's now confront a good number of teachers, and the provision of at least some authentic support can make a great difference. Teachers can be faced with actual calls for help from their pupils. We heard from a teacher in another secondary school group who told how two Asian girls — bags packed and about to run away from their severely restrictive homes — implored her to help them. In the nursery and infant school, teachers may meet second- and third-generation 'immigrant' children with emotional problems whose mothers, having rejected their own mothers' foreign culture in adolescence, lack acceptable maternal support now that they are mothers themselves and are struggling with severe depressions. Teresa's teachers have not, I think, just been 'lucky' with their results. There seemed to be grounds for hope, as is suggested elsewhere (Meltzer, 1979), that the timely support, which they had at first been unable to give because they did not understand her provocations, may have helped her to cope and care not only in the present, but also in future. (For the practice of pastoral care for Asian girls, see Pelleschi (1985).)

Don
Don was presented at the second meeting of a group of a dozen teachers from three infant and junior schools on one site, later to be joined by secondary school intake staff, and was the third case considered. Two junior school teachers had presented cases of two boys at the first meeting, had begun to try out some of the ideas produced during the discussion and had reported that the boys had begun to respond to them better already, one being 'now a changed boy'. It seemed necessary therefore for me to sound a note of caution against expecting such sudden changes in every case or mistaking quick changes for permanent solutions. Mrs. B. then presented the case of this 8-year-old in the top class of the infant school.

She was greatly concerned about his inability to cope at all in class. She said that he did not listen to explanations, was convinced that he 'can't do' whatever she required and, when she coaxed him, would sob for great lengths of time. He wanted her to sit beside him all the time, stopped working if she left him and did not believe her when she said 'I know you can do it'. Although he did not find writing difficult and liked to write in her presence, he wanted to play all the time, which she allowed him to do as far as possible, while feeling very uneasy about giving him special treatment so below his age. The group asked about his background. Mrs. B. described an all-female home with quite a strong-willed unsupported West Indian mother who worked outside the home until late in the day. A teenage sister acted as mother substitute and collected Don and his 6-year-old sister from school every afternoon. The younger sister was herself very naughty at school and teased her older brother mercilessly in public. It seemed that when he was younger he had been left with child-minders who were unable to meet his early need for play, which would account for his wanting to play now. Thinking about his desolate sobbing, the group were guided to speculate about his possible depression. He was always among seemingly powerful women at home and at school (the school had an all-female staff), and defenceless even against the taunts of a younger sister. Was he getting any support in 'being a boy'? Since there were at least some happier moments during the day when he could succeed (as in his writing), could such situations be multiplied, perhaps through some link with his play? Could he be 'caught at being successful', helped to be helpful and then rewarded with permission to do what he liked best? Could there be some exchange of information, at least occasionally, with his busy mother, to see whether she might be able to find at least a little time daily just for him?

At the end of the meeting, Mrs. B. confessed her relief that there had been no suggestion of not letting him play but that his play might be linked to learning activities. She now had a number of ideas for this and for some contact with the mother.

A few weeks later, Mrs. B. reported that Don had begun to respond, and that an exciting additional development had arisen from the first discussion, which involved another member of the group, Mr. G. from the junior school to which Don would proceed 9 months later. Following the discussion of Don's difficulties, this teacher had offered, with the agreement of his headteacher, to meet a small group of boys in the infant school, including Don, once a week for various activities. The offer had been gratefully accepted (and proved such a success that the school decided at the end of the year to fill a vacant post with a male teacher). For Don, that group became the highlight of the week. He became more outgoing in the company of his male peers, started to organise and speed up 'his' group to be in time for Mr. G.; his progress there was linked with the learning activities in his classroom at which he had hitherto failed.

One result of Don's improvement also led the teachers' group to consider an apparently peculiar feature of classroom dynamics.

Martin
Martin, who had been 'good' when Don was in trouble, now seemed to have taken over Don's role. Other teachers immediately mentioned similar experiences and were encouraged to explore what seemed to be happening in such situations. They were offered some group theory as to how a role which is relinquished by one member of a group will be assigned to another if the group needed someone to carry it. They

related this to the dynamics of the class–teacher relationship and asked themselves what parts they might be playing in the constellation of their classes, what the implications were for the management of the situation and how they could help the children to achieve eventual autonomy and the ability to withstand group pressures.

Mrs. B. then thought that she was herself contributing to this new difficulty in her vexation. There seemed to be a regular sequence. Martin would make an unreasonable demand (e.g. to read to the headteacher at an inconvenient moment); Mrs. B. would feel that he was trying it on and would answer shortly 'no, you can't.' Martin would start upsetting the other children, and she would then try to mitigate her rejection by being nice to him. She had now become aware of her inconsistency and how she had unintentionally kindled the trouble through being irritated by this new difficulty and had then rewarded disruptive behaviour; so she began to find ways of making necessary refusals less total (e.g. she would say, 'You can't read to Mrs. M. now, but we'll ask her if she can see you when you have finished your bit of writing. It's ever so nice what you have been doing.').

The aim of these discussions was not only to increase the teachers' insight into the cases presented but also to introduce them to the kind of questions which might enable them to find workable solutions to the problems of the classroom. This requires a certain amount of direction in the early stages. Both groups illustrate how a consultant's initially high profile can start this process, generate ideas in response to a need better understood and lead from the case in question into issues which are important for teaching in general.

In neither case did the directiveness take the form of advice on how to handle the pupil, as the teachers had originally expected. Instead, they were involved in exploring alternatives and in making their own decisions about them. In both groups they accepted, with considerable relief in one case, the consultant's expectation that they would use their own judgement with regard to the questions raised. Both groups were able to appreciate quite soon the possibility of unintentionally reinforcing a child's problematic behaviour by the teacher's own reaction to it. They discovered how to use this *self-awareness* to good purpose, both in response to a child's immediate need and in the service of long-term educational objectives.

Both cases also had their *inter-school* aspects, directly so in Don's case where immediate inter-school activity came to benefit him and other children, and as an issue to be considered, at least, in Teresa's case.

How groups develop their expertise from case to case

(i) Development of skills in a three-term inter-school primary staff group (from Don and Martin, to Michael to Vic)

Don and Martin

By the end of the first term, the teachers who had been concerned with Don and Martin had accepted that, even with consultation, problems would not go away overnight and had got used to not being advised what to do and to exploring the issues instead, in order to be able to find workable solutions. Although the questions asked by the consultant and colleagues in the group, and the ideas produced in response, tended to be transformed into something like advice, this tendency decreased in the course of the term. The children discussed were no longer presenting the teachers with 'insoluble' problems, and the group finished the first term on such an optimistic note that they invited another infant school, whose children proceeded to one of the junior schools already represented, to join them.

Michael

Michael's teacher, Mrs. C., belonged to this fourth school, which had not, like the others, actually asked for help with disturbed children but had gladly accepted the invitation to join the group.

The issue of seemingly unhelpful parents and home situations had come up in most of the cases discussed. It complicated Michael's case in a different but equally poignant way. After attending a few of these discussions in the group's second term, Mrs. C. presented Michael: 6 years old, very anxious in new situations, tearful and panicky at everything that he was asked to do for himself, even if well within his ability, refusing to eat unless Mrs. C. sat beside him, soiling himself unless she took him to the toilet and scratching other children when they claimed her attention. To the group, his fears and uncertainty about his own adequacy seemed likely to have something to do with the father's lack of time for the family, his disregard of the boy and his preference for the younger sister, which the mother had mentioned to the teacher. The group then discussed whether the child's feelings of self-worth could be enhanced in small steps during the school day and whether the mother, who seemed to let the boy control her by his 'helplessness', might be induced to do likewise.

Mrs. C., still new to the group, did not participate in this discussion but listened thoughtfully. As we heard later, she attempted both strategies. She had hesitated for some time to broach the subject with the mother but eventually did so in one of their chats at the school gate, suggesting that it might help Michael if his father could be persuaded to spend about 15 minutes a day playing with him and making him feel important. Although the mother was at first loath to bring the topic up at home, the discussion seemed to have had some effect. A few weeks later, Mrs. C. told the group that Michael — who had never talked about home at school — had begun to talk to her about his dad, and how he had played football with him. He was also becoming less tense and more self-reliant, all of which seemed to Mrs. C. like a sort of miracle. She congratulated the mother accordingly.

The following term, however, Mrs. C. reported that Michael was 'losing his spark'. When she cautiously mentioned this to the mother, she heard that, when she told her husband about Michael's improvement at school, he stopped spending time with him 'since he was all right now'! Mrs. C. then encouraged the mother to impress on her husband how important he still was for the boy, hoping that this would induce him to give Michael some attention during the coming summer holidays.

In talking about Michael during the spring and summer terms, the group, again, had discussed much more than a sequence of events. The poignancy of the experience made them explore how badly *parents* can underestimate their significance to their children and what *teachers* can do — even in face of initial resistance — to encourage them to support their children more actively. They examined how one also needs to respect the complexities of family relationships and must not push advice. This had helped Mrs. C., a newcomer to the group, to become less afraid of 'seeming to pry' and had enabled her to make effective suggestions as she and the mother exchanged information about the child. The group as a whole had shown and commented on their growing self-confidence in seizing opportunities for such exchanges. They found that this often gave results, especially when the problem seemed to be lack of understanding rather than a deeper disturbance in family relationships. Even in more serious cases, parents seemed to gain something from sharing anxieties with the teacher, as we shall see when this group turns its attention to Vic.

It is also of interest that, as a group develop their skills in exploring the underlying issues, *newcomers* are able to benefit from their earlier explorations and from the questions that the members have learnt to ask themselves, from their awareness and from actions reflecting the stage reached by the group as a whole. (It had been a special feature of this group that, alongside core members attending throughout the course, short-term members attended for half a term, or even once only for special cases, to give as many of the staff the opportunity to attend as wanted to.) Like newcomers, short-term members, as we shall see with Vic's teacher, seemed to catch up quite quickly with the stages of the core group that preceded their arrival. This resembled what workers in the related fields of counselling and psychotherapy report as *special features of brief attendance*, when limited time may encourage a feeling of urgency.

Vic

Concurrently with the summer term follow-up on Michael, Vic's teacher, Miss D., had brought up the difficulties that the school had with this 7-year-old.

Vic had been 'destructive from the first moment that he joined the school' in his third year and 'in trouble every day', 'hated everybody', 'had no interest in anything' and always demanded immediate attention; bright but underachieving, he concentrated only on things that he knew he could do, such as easy first-year work. He had no friends, kicked other children, ripped up work-cards and swore loudly at his teacher, who had 'tried everything' without success and despairingly would now be 'glad to see the back of him'. The mother had moved into the area on remarriage. The step-father, apparently on good terms with the boy before the marriage and academically ambitious for him, had in the meantime lost patience with him and begun to compare him unfavourably with his own two children, who lived with their mother. He was now treating him severely while his troublesome behaviour grew worse and he began to bully his step-siblings when they met. The school then learnt from the mother that her husband was threatening to leave her unless she got rid of Vic. Most unhappy about this but wanting to save her marriage, she was now wondering whether 'to let Vic go into care'. Things had got so bad between the parents that a child-minding neighbour was now helping to rescue Vic by taking him into her own house, away from the strife.

Vic had first been discussed in the previous term, at an *ad hoc* meeting with the whole staff of the school. This discussion had helped the teacher that he then had to improve the relationship between them, but she had to leave the school and Vic had to adjust to a new teacher. Miss D., an alert, committed, young probationer, had been present at the earlier discussion and could therefore now 'tune in' to

Vic's behaviour. However, the child clearly found the change of teacher very upsetting, and a colleague of hers, a core member of the inter-school group on the site, invited her to talk about these difficulties in the group.

Miss D. told us how, when Vic refused to work for her, she 'bent over backwards' to help him, even in his worst tantrums, using a strategy of giving in constructively (such as letting him play with the gerbils). She was resentful, however, that her headteacher kept coming into the room to see how Vic was getting on and to tell her to handle him more firmly. As she did not believe in this, she could not make it work. As a result she had begun to hate the whole situation, especially since Vic, having sensed the disagreement between Miss D. and the Headteacher, had now begun to ask to move to another class, that of Mrs. X. This made Miss D. feel even more inadequate and unhappy, both 'hating' Vic for this and feeling like putting her arm round him to comfort him — feelings which the mother had also spoken of when telling the headteacher how Vic was spoiling her marriage. Aware how much Miss D. minded Vic's rebuff of her efforts and love, I was able at this point to draw the group's attention to other resemblances between the adults at home and those at school in their relationships with Vic. He had lost a father who, he had once said, 'was better than (his) new Dad' and had lost a teacher who had begun to understand him. Mother and 'new Dad', on the one hand, and the headteacher and Miss D., on the other, also disagreed on how he should be treated, which, at home, meant rescue by the neighbour; so perhaps Vic was trying to reproduce this solution by asking to move to another teacher's class.

This apparent *re-enactment* by the staff of what was happening at home, and the child's similar response to it, could now be discussed at one of the last meetings, which the headteacher also attended. Seeing it as the far from rare phenomenon of an 'unwitting professional response' (Britton, 1981) helped to ensure that there would be no loss of face over the disagreement between colleagues (especially colleagues of such disparate status as the headteacher and a probationary teacher). It was possible first to explore in general the anxieties of committed professionals, irrespective of their length of experience and professional status, when faced with such harrowing cases as Vic's, and how easily these can lead to staff disagreements which may resemble those at home. We then looked at how teachers who become aware that their anxieties reflect those of the children can use this insight to help them to understand themselves better. Miss D. could herself give an example of this: she had, in the meantime, had a chat with Vic, explaining that she, too, had sometimes to do as she was told, even if she did not quite want to, and how angry this can make one feel. This seemed to have made a deep impression on him and may have helped him to identify with her. She spoke of a much better relationship with him since then; she was herself more relaxed with him, and he was doing better work and no longer asked to move to another class. All this the headteacher was able to confirm. The headteacher also told the group that she had previously advised the mother to seek help from the child guidance clinic. The mother had already been much helped by the support that she had received from the school following their discussions and no longer wished to send Vic away; she said that she now knew that it was not Vic who needed guidance, but she and her husband. She had therefore contacted the Marriage Guidance Council and already felt that her marriage was beginning to improve.

This case discussion, by an inter-school group whose core members had now met for nearly three terms, demonstrates what consultancy can do for a school both within and across its boundaries.

It shows with what sophistication such a group can approach a child's apparently intractable situation, as they gradually deepen their understanding of such children's needs and of how they can meet these better. Vic, who hated everybody, could nevertheless be seen as in need of benign authority to help him to bear his feelings of anger and depression when threatened with the consequences of his parents' problems. the teachers could be helped to understand his needs better by the support that they themselves received in relation to their own anxieties about the way that they handled him and the way that they worked together as colleagues within the institutional hierarchy and across the school boundaries. Learning not to reproduce the dynamics of a child's home situation, they could give Vic the new learning experiences which he needed and provide enough support to a despairing parent to prevent her making a perhaps irreversible decision (like giving her child into care) out of despair. She was enabled to think again and to seek the kind of help which made such a decision unnecessary.

In this case, too, newcomers to a group (including the secondary school's intake staff), even at this advanced stage of its existence, were able to benefit from the support which the group had developed and the questions that members were asking themselves.

(ii) Development of skills in a two-term inter-school primary staff group (from Tony to Dave and Jeanie (three consecutive case discussions))

As to the phenomenon of re-enactment as an unwitting professional response, the reader is referred to current discussion (Britton, 1981) of how difficult it is for professionals to resist such a response and how detrimentally failure to do so affects the help they could otherwise give. As we saw in Vic's case discussion, the processes which can be activated in staff group consultation can contribute to awareness of these issues. This can sometimes develop quite early in the life of a group. Dave's case illustrates another aspect of such unwitting re-enactment; here the pupil's difficult behaviour was reflected in the presentation itself and discussion of his problems.

We now rejoin the staff of Tony's school (p. 14–18) as they explore how one might help Dave and Jeanie.

Dave, 'an infuriating boy, who never listens and who cannot even copy from the board'
Dave's case was presented a week after we had discussed Tony's in their fourth meeting. We saw how at the previous meeting the whole group had rallied round Mrs. A., had identified with her concern for him and had followed the direction of my 'thinking aloud'. With the exception of the previous session, Dave's teacher, Mr. E., had seemed set — through his frequent 'yes, but . . .' interjections — to become the group's resident 'butter-in', trying to keep the talk at the level of breezy non-concern. With remarks like 'Ah well, that never did me any harm', he would brush aside his colleagues' explorations as irrelevant but now and then throw into the discussion quite harrowing details about early bereavement in his own life. Such personal comments, as we shall see later, cannot be taken up in a professional staff support group, since they are outside its brief and scope. Yet we know that our personal experience can have an effect on our reactions to others and, in the case of a teacher, on his reactions to his pupils and his demands on them. It was with this background in mind that I listened to Mr. E.'s description of Dave.

Eight years old, now in his second term at this school, Dave was exasperatingly 'lazy', always talking to others, the only one in the class who will make a mess of things, who cannot even copy from the board, but who can sometimes surprise by good work. He never listens, just switches off, does the opposite from what he is told and underachieves in everything. Mr. E. finds it hard to understand, comparing him with his 'hard-working, extremely bright sister' who is 1 year older, how there can be two such different children in one family. He quotes the mother as confirming that Dave is an infuriating boy, so different from his clever and hard-working sister.

At this point, the group asks for further information, clearly trying to dig for any positive features in Dave that had been hinted at but buried in Mr. E.'s account. When asked about the surprisingly good work, he could not remember, and this lapse of memory made him thoughtful. The group then recalled their own experiences with children who refused to work and how often there seemed to be another child in the family who 'cannot do anything wrong'. They gave examples of how some of their attempts at building up self-esteem seemed to have worked. Mr. E., however, countered each example with either 'it wouldn't work with Dave' or 'I've tried all this', and switched off at any good idea offered, unable to listen, making himself, like Dave, the only one in the group who was so different. He eventually induced in the group a feeling of hopelessness, which must have resembled what both Mr. E. and Dave were feeling in the classroom.

Having so far remained silent in the discussion, I decided not to point this out at this stage. Instead, I used the device of the 'relevant tale' (Caplan, 1970), a true example of how fanning small positive sparks in seemingly totally negative behaviour can make a difference. I related an incident from another group of a teacher who, like Mr. E., had noticed a tiny potential for better behaviour (Mr. E. had done this but had only used it to prove that Dave could do better if he tried, as exasperated teachers often do). The teacher of the tale, however, had used this potential in a matter-of-fact manner to give the pupil hope about himself rather than to confirm his despair.

The 'tale' was intended to deflect attention from Mr. E. at the moment of the group's hopelessness about him and to remind him instead of his own buried awareness of the boy's potential, by illustrating a way out of the vicious circle of perpetual defeat. This lead the group to recall, at the end of the meeting, how they had obtained better results when they had worked on the relationship with a work-refusing child, instead of constantly demanding better work, which had got them nowhere, as with Dave (thus identifying with Mr. E. as having known failure instead of contrasting their own 'better' results with his, as they had done earlier).

At the next meeting, Mr. E. almost casually mentioned that he had been trying out one or two of last week's ideas and that Dave surprisingly seemed quite responsive to him this week. He was now showing his own responsiveness to Dave and Dave's response to that, which made Mr. E. more hopeful about him. This seemed a better moment to comment on last week's parallels between the interaction of the group and Mr. E., and the teacher–pupil interaction which he had described — how Mr. E. had played Dave's part in the group, who thus experienced what it was like to have a Dave in the class and responded to him as if he were Dave, feeling hopeless at his apparent refusal to consider their ideas. This the group found fascinating, especially Mr. E. who now saw how this had happened, and several times referred to it in later sessions. In one of these he reported laughingly how he had involved another colleague in such discussion when he had caught both himself and the colleague 'fixing' another child inadvertently in his bad behaviour. Equally important, he felt that he was managing to convey something of his greater hopefulness to Dave's mother, who in turn seemed to be becoming more accepting. While Dave was still a problem, it now seemed to him remediable. It no longer aroused feelings of exasperation, as it had done when he had failed to link what had amounted to a form of work paralysis with the hopelessness which Dave must have felt about himself both at home and at school.

This discussion — in sequence — exemplifies the different ways in which a consultant can exercise the role.

In contrast with my somewhat directive involvement during the previous session (Tony's case discussion), I had said very little, apart from using the 'relevant tale', whose functions were to divert attention from Mr. E.'s hopelessness while helping the group to support him — not by recounting their own success stories but by recognising what support potential he might already have, ready to be drawn out by support from others. This helped him to behave likewise with a failing pupil, so that both he and the child had less need to make others feel useless. His report suggested that he had made a beginning in that direction.

As has been found in training groups with doctors (Gosling, 1965) and social workers (Irvine, 1959), the teacher's 'impersonation' of the pupil evoked his own response in the group, giving them a taste of what it was like to be that pupil's teacher. The consultant tried to help the group to share these feelings and then to overcome them, instead of being overwhelmed, as the teacher had been. In this context the 'relevant incident' was used as a teaching technique.

The case also illustrates the need for carefully timing comments on the reflection of the situation in the classroom. As we shall see later, such timing must depend on the effect that the comments seem likely to have on the discussion. Had I made these comments while Mr. E. was still feeling helpless they would not have been helpful, as they were when he had become more hopeful and his experience could be looked at as a whole. It was more acceptable to wait until feelings had cooled before drawing attention to what it had felt like for Mr. E. to be behaving like Dave, and for the group to be getting nowhere, as Mr. E. was with Dave, and using this to illuminate the problem between teacher and child. As Mr. E. began to understand and respect the pupil's feelings behind his refusal to work, he could also relax his pressure.

In this way, he and his colleagues found it possible to recognise when their own behaviour was self-defeating, which is notoriously not facilitated by criticism. It was brought about through the group process, which enabled Mr. E. to relax his hold on his preconceived ideas about Dave and about his own ineffectiveness with him. He could now have a fresh look at the situation, seeing it also from the pupil's point of view, and respond more appropriately to the needs indicated by the boy's behaviour. Only then was Mr. E. able to make demands on Dave in such a way that the boy could begin to meet them.

Jeanie

The following week, the group discussed Jeanie — a girl in Tony's class — whose difficulties, of growing concern to her teacher, Mrs. A., were also involving Mrs. A. with a social worker with whom she disagreed.

It tends to be the client — in the case of children the child and parents — who suffers when there are such *interprofessional dis-agreements*, wounded feelings or attempts to defend challenged competences (Hornby, 1983). These hazards could be tackled in good time by Mrs. A., who was wondering how to help this 9-year-old in her crippled relationships with others.

Jeanie so irritated everybody with her fussy attention-seeking helpfulness that others found her unbearable and no one in the class wanted to work or play with her. This worsened with every new attempt that she made to be helpful. Fostered since babyhood, but not freed for adoption by her alcoholic mother who met her at irregular intervals, Jeanie seemed happy with her foster parents but frightened that she might become 'mad' like her mother. According to her foster mother, she also feared the frequent visits of the social worker, to whom she could not relate.

The teacher could see that there was a difficulty, as the social worker had not wanted her to discuss Jeanie in our support group or with him, since according to her he did not think that teachers are qualified to deal with such cases. He had apparently told the foster mother that the child should be seen by a psychiatrist, to which the foster mother had reacted with shock, feeling that she had failed Jeanie. She had spoken to Mrs. A. about this in a frank and caring way, which had strengthened Mrs. A.'s impression that no child could be in better foster care than Jeanie. She had tried to convey this to the foster mother, recalling Jeanie's happy accounts of her relationship with her.

After this account the group was helped to explore whether Jeanie could be guided towards a less obtrusive helpfulness and whether some of the more mature children in the class could be encouraged to be more friendly when working in a group with her. The group were also asked to examine what opportunities there were for foster mother, social worker and school to exchange information in such a way that all sides could listen to each other and explore what Jeanie really needed.

A few weeks later, Mrs. A. reported that this strategy was begin-ning to work, that Jeanie was responding and that 'a lot was now going for her'. Mrs. A. also felt that the discussion had helped her to give more support to the foster mother by tentatively exploring with her Jeanie's anxieties and possible feelings of guilt towards her own mother, who wanted to be with her but had to leave her after each brief encounter, and by saying that a caring foster mother such as her was bound to be a tremendous support. She had suggested that Jeanie might like to talk to her foster mother about these things and that it might also be a good idea for teacher and foster mother to include the social worker in their next discussion.

The group then heard that the headteacher of the school was inviting the social worker and the foster parents to meet herself and the class teacher. This enabled the group to consider beforehand the possible implications of the disagreements between teacher and social worker, alerting the teacher to the hazards of interprofessional rivalry and to her opportunity to handle them with sensitivity. Mrs. A., encouraged by Jeanie's good response to her strategies, felt that referral to yet another agency seemed inappropriate at this moment, as it might reinforce the child's feeling of being unacceptably different, which was already underlined by the social worker's frequent visits. She therefore decided to suggest that things could be left to tick over for a while; she and the foster parents would see what evolved as they built on the insights gained. Thus the social worker's suggestion of referral would not be rejected but postponed. Mrs. A. then agreed with the social worker that help through child guidance should be offered after the ground had been prepared, depending on what needs emerged as both home and school worked together along the lines agreed. Social services agreed that their worker's visits might, in the meantime, be less frequent.

All this paid dividends; the teacher's sensitive attempt to overcome the disagreement between the social worker and herself prevented it from escalating into defensive insistence on premature suggestions from either side, it also heightened the foster mother's confidence in her relationship with Jeanie and it helped Jeanie directly and indirectly. A couple of weeks later, Mrs. A. reported that Jeanie was now rather more relaxed with the others in her class, had begun to talk to Mrs. A. about her 'two Mums' and allowed more access to her thoughts and feelings.

In this group, as in others which contain teachers from several schools serving the same community, there also arose a particular benefit as a result of the inter-school setting. Meeting colleagues from other schools (both infant, junior and secondary) in the neighbour-hood, they may find that some members of the group have previously taught the child presented or may be teaching one or more siblings and know their parents, so that they may be able to add something about the family situation. When the child's former teachers hear about his/her problems in the present school and gain increased understanding, they are likely to view some of their present pupils differently or may be able to give some anticipatory guidance before a pupil proceeds to the next school.

In Jeanie's case, her former infant school teacher learnt in the group how the child's difficulties — which the teacher had wrongly hoped she would grow out of — had increased with age; she commented at the end of the discussion that it was clearly not sufficient just to hope for improvements and that unobtrusive help is best given as early as possible. The group process had activated a better understanding of the irritating child and of how easily one provides such attention-seekers with justification for their fears of rejection by rejecting them afresh with each manifestation of their craving for acceptance. The group members also became more aware of how the vicious circle might be broken by paying more attention at an early stage to the desired behaviour.

(iii) Two case discussions of a two-term intra-school secondary staff group (John and Dipak)

Disagreement between professionals occurs, as we know, across as well as within institutions, and can enrich professional life as much as it sometimes frustrates it. Hazards are more likely when there is insufficient exchange of information and no systematic discussion of experience between colleagues — a risk known to most secondary school staffs in particular. Since they have to deal for much shorter periods with the difficulties of many more pupils, they may easily not be aware of how any one pupil's problems assume significantly different manifestations with different teachers. We saw how much better Teresa's teachers understood and began to support her after they had systematically explored the various, seemingly contradictory, experiences that they had with her. Such exchange of unclouded information about a difficult pupil can be particularly useful to both pupil and teachers in the case of those whose aggressive behaviour appears to challenge everything that teachers represent and to refuse even the best-intentioned efforts to help them to progress.

John
John dared his teachers to hit him and threatened to thump them if they did.

He was a mathematically gifted 15-year-old who had managed within 14 months to be demoted from the top mathematics set down to the sixth, doing increasingly less work after each demotion. Promised promotion if he worked hard, he still came bottom in each new set, in spite of the ability that he had shown. He had also become insolent, sneered at teachers when spoken to and was sent out of classrooms because of his aggressive behaviour. However, he did get on well with some teachers, such as the physics mistress, who managed to deflect his behaviour with jocular retorts which he liked, and with two of the men teachers whom he had at first challenged with the same stubborn defiance but to whose firm friendliness he was now responding.

His parents were divorced, the two children split between them, and John lived with his father and step-mother but, when in trouble, secretly sought comfort from his mother, which the father tried to prevent. However, this knowledge alone had not helped the teachers to deal with John constructively.

We therefore focused on the teachers' differing experiences with him and on what his different reactions might suggest about his needs and how to meet them. An important question which arose was whether teachers do not have a choice in how they react to the difficulties that we all experience when we teach rejecting pupils who treat us with aggression and provocation. We looked at how such feelings can develop — how years of parental strife might for instance have set John a bad example as regards the management of aggression and have aroused chaotic feelings with no help in dealing with them. Was John perhaps 'testing' his teachers for their ability to control that chaos, wanting confrontations but needing people to set limits without rejecting him? He seemed to become 'teachable' with teachers who asserted authority firmly but not punitively, whom he could not goad into the aggressiveness which he himself felt towards authority figures and who could see in him not a boy who challenged their authority but a boy who needed their guidance into adulthood, whose 'bluff' they could call jocularly but without ridicule and whose 'reality' they appreciated. Any other responses, such as the retaliation that the other teachers had reported, would feel to him like adult pretence which he had to challenge; where he was not victorious in this way, however, he seemed to be able to settle down quite happily to serious work. This seemed to happen with teachers who refused to confirm his view of himself as an unacceptable person, who passed the test of setting him limits without feeling they had conquered an opponent (Winnicott, 1965) but who knew that they had achieved something on his behalf.

The two main questions to consider were how to deal constructively with behaviour like John's and how to do so in the face of severe provocation in public, when one is under pressure to remain in charge.

Could one, for instance, use the time that John forced them to spend in conflict with him differently, talk with him about his anger, show that one understood it and tentatively reflect his feelings back to him, i.e. show him that one accepted his reasons for feeling angry but that he must not act it out, that he, too, sometimes managed to control his anger and that that was an achievement in the right direction? Could one also talk to him about the anger which he incited in others and about how this can make people unfair? Could one make him understand that his own unfairness towards others and theirs towards him were almost inevitable if he went on provoking them? Could he be helped to recognise how lonely anger can make people and how this could be avoided by taking a hold on himself, as he had shown that he could? Could one work out a strategy that encouraged him to work at self-control and at accepting responsibility for his behaviour, by frequent feedback on small and partial successes, while his unacceptable behaviour was firmly controlled? This would be to set him limits, while also protecting and building on what was 'good' in him, thereby giving him hope about himself by putting him in touch with the more mature parts of his self?

When the teachers were looking at John's behaviour in that light it was also possible to ask them to look at the choice that we ourselves have in the ways in which we look at others, especially those who defy us. We considered that such choice may have something to do with our own blind spots and that we might deal with these by trying to recall how our own powerful aggressions in childhood had been brought under control: we may then find remnants of our past experience of control in the temptation to respond aggressively now to pupils' provocations.

What I was suggesting was that, if we can learn that much about ourselves, it may be possible to deal with these remnants and prevent them from interfering with our professional skills, thus becoming more effective in teaching children whose desperation is expressed in aggressive behaviour, and that anger uncomplicated by such childhood residues will be of a different quality and more likely to produce the desired result than if it arises from our own insecurity, which we hate to be exposed.

Relieved that anger in the classroom need not be seen as unprofessional and totally condemnable and that some anger could be accepted as well placed and educative, the teachers then started to examine what opportunities one might create in the curriculum for helping young people such as John to understand and to handle angry feelings and the range of emotions that they are trying to come to grips with and to develop capacities for enriching relationships. They found that the whole range of subjects which they taught between them (social studies, English, art, mathematics, science, PE, French, 'child care and personality', commerce and remedial education) would lend itself, in content or method of approach, to such possibility (as we shall examine in a later section).

All the members took an active, thoughtful part in these explorations, relating them to John and to the many others with such problems, but only a few of his teachers belonged to the group, which was concerned about those who had not taken part in the discussion. It was suggested that 'daughter groups' should be formed with his other teachers to enable them to confer systematically about appropriate strategies and about any further needs which emerged.

However, John reached a new crisis before this could be implemented, and his tutor (who had presented his case) pleaded with his seniors for John to be given another chance. Without further discussion with all those concerned in what this implied, the plea led to John's sudden promotion by two sets in mathematics as a sign of goodwill and to show confidence that he could do better. Unfortunately this involved a complete change of teachers; he lost not only those with whom he had had the worst confrontations but also those whom he had liked and those who had learned to understand him better and had begun to expect him to respond differently. The 'new chance' may have looked to him like rejection by those that he had taken to, so that the intended encouragement turned into loss for him. There had been no time for discussion with the new teachers of how the transition might best be handled and of the fears and hopes involved. Some of these teachers had seen his promotion as rewarding bad behaviour, so that his old reputation and the expectations attached to it preceded him. These expectations of trouble then fulfilled themselves, John's behaviour got worse, and his father was advised to move him to another school.

This was a painful lesson for the group but, although John was now beyond the reach of these teachers' better understanding, later cases had the benefit of it where lack of communication between staff might allow institutional processes to take the wrong course.

In all their following case discussions, and with cases not discussed, it became a matter of course to think of opportunities also in the curriculum which could help the teachers to combine their educational and enabling functions. They had found it useful to share and discuss their different reactions and ways of handling a provocative pupil and how to deflect his aggression instead of 'fixing' it with that 'fatal seriousness' (Erikson, 1980) with which adults frequently respond to adolescents' experimental stances.

Dipak
This benefitted Dipak, a fourth-form Indian boy, who was the next case presented. A shudder went through the group when his name was mentioned. Teachers had come to reject him for the 'creepy manner' with which he 'pestered' them with whining complaints and requests for special permission to come late, to leave early or not to attend games. By these means he hoped to avoid the other boys, whose bullying he attracted. With no friends in or out of school, he constantly sought help, mainly from women teachers — the men teachers, he

said, frightened him. The women felt drained by his continuous waylaying and tried to cut him short when they could not fend him off or avoid him altogether; they could not bear his irritating manner.

He was, however, hardworking, especially in his mathematics set and quite imaginitive in social studies. His work looked beautiful but was academically of a very poor quality and quite out of line with his grandiose ideas about his future; mad on aeroplanes, he wanted to become a pilot, from which his teachers tried in vain to dissuade him because of his poor work.

The teachers had little knowledge about his family, as his father spoke no English and his mother was living in India.

Teachers had tried to sympathise with him in the past but categorically refused to do so any longer; bullying had been dealt with, at senior level, as a racial issue, which the teachers did not think it was, since they felt that Dipak created his own problems. What had now lost him the teachers' sympathies was that 'he lied to us about a holiday in India' when he had simply played truant.

The partly nervous, partly hostile rejection of the boy in the group seemed total. They were unwilling to look for any positive features from which to start their exploration and demanded solutions from me, as definite as those which Dipak seemed to want from his teachers. I offered them none and they felt left in the lurch — as one could suppose that Dipak felt.

As the lie about the holiday in India appeared to constitute the point at which Dipak lost all sympathy, it seemed appropriate to deflect the discussion from Dipak to feelings which people have when lied to. These ranged from anger at being thought stupid enough to fall for it to outrage at the violation of deeply felt morals; but, I asked, were these always the intentions behind lies? Although people who lied did often want to get away with things, was lying not also frequently a defence against emotional difficulties or even a build-up of fantasies to bridge a seemingly unbridgeable ('unthinkable') gap between wish and reality? What if this particular lie, from a lonely boy, were such a fantasy, coupled perhaps with an illusion that fantasies can make the wish come true? What was this fantasy about, if not being where his mother was? Might there be some link between the missing, longed-for, mother and his constant attempts to get help from the women teachers?

As the group followed this train of thought, they spoke again of his obsession with aeroplanes and the pilot fantasy now fitting into this picture. They accepted that terms such as 'liar' were better discarded as unhelpful labels which interfered with attempts at understanding people.

By eliminating the lie as a justification for rejection, the group could now focus on the boy's likely feelings and how the world must look to him; frightened of others in and outside school, he hoped that women teachers at least would understand and yet was unable to make them listen or relate to him, and he set about this in the most unsuitable way, possibly for want of any better experience at home in how to forge relationships.

It so happened that in earlier meetings there had been several references to the frustration that the teachers themselves felt when they were not listened to by their superiors. They had also felt let down by me when I did not give them the solutions that they demanded. I was therefore able to link this part of Dipak's experience with their own; not to be listened to by authority, whose job it should be to listen, was clearly very upsetting to most people. If, as they had said, Dipak was creating his own problems by the way in which he approached people, did that not happen to most of us? When we expect not to be listened to, do we express ourselves less well, appear to be demanding and thus help to create or reinforce the failure in communication? Had they not, for instance, allowed their seniors to treat Dipak's situation as one of racial bullying, although they themselves had thought there was more to it, so that impairment of his personal relationships, due to other factors, remained untackled?

With John's case in mind, the group then suggested that Dipak needed tutorial arrangements in addition to the existing academic ones, that he needed a focal point in the institution and that — in the light of his personal situation, and considering the kind of teachers that he was seeking out — there should be a woman tutor able to adapt her professional skills to his special needs, both to shelter and to stretch him. There were, after all, points in his work on which one could build, so that he could begin to feel a bit more accepted and thereby perhaps he could learn to accept himself more. Could such a tutor not also try to develop in him some social skills, help him to understand the reactions of others and see to it that, in class, group work was designed in such a way that he could practise such skills, especially if it involved those of his interests (e.g. aeroplanes) which others would be able to share?

Miss F., who made these suggestions, obviously saw how this could be initiated, and the group felt that, if she were to be Dipak's tutor, she would need his other teachers to fall in with her strategies. There would clearly be no easy way to achieve all this, considering what strong prejudice there now was against the boy; their own jittery reaction in the group, the derision and shudders with which they had earlier corroborated and extended details of the description had perhaps shown something of the social unconscious in relation to the features that they saw in him. They had at first, by their insistent demand for an immediate solution, hardly allowed me to help them to explore his case, which had made me feel momentarily as useless as the boy made them feel!

We could now understand that Dipak had multiple difficulties: his mother's permanent absence; a home and school with a great gulf between their cultures; perhaps a general rejection by the community. I reminded them of their own negative *in*capability earlier in the discussion and their irritable demands for quick solutions in a manner which implied that none could be found. (I had referred to Keats (letter, 21 December 1817) who referred to negative capability as 'when a man is capable of being in uncertainties, mysteries, doubts, without any irritable reaching after fact and reason . . .'.) More aware of their reactions to the boy's difficulties, they could now see these reactions as no longer totally alien to their own experience. They had seen for themselves how selective one's perceptions can be and how one tends to note behaviour which confirms one's constructs and to ignore or barely to notice behaviour which contradicts such constructs but which might, if observed, transform rejection into acceptance and help to repair damaged relationships. Aware of how they themselves were reproaching their superiors for behaving towards them as they behaved towards a pupil, they were able to appreciate that they were, on the one hand, adding to his hopelessness and, on the other, increasing their own frustration within the hierarchy.

Somewhat bemused by these turns in their preconceptions, the teachers decided to try Miss F.'s suggestions. She later reported that Dipak was responding to her approach and was beginning to be less tense with some other boys at least.

While examining Dipak's situation, we had also looked at the feelings which 'pupils whom one cannot teach' can generate and considered how these can lead to irritable demands on others — on pupils, on colleagues in the institutional hierarchy and, in this case, also on the outside consultant. These demands are often made in a way which can make those to whom they are addressed feel useless or hostile. We had thus taken John's case further by looking more closely at relations and communications in the institution itself and at the quality of the members' own negotiating skills when things were going wrong between teachers and pupils, between the pupils themselves or between colleagues. These are of course the issues emphasised by those who consult on individual problems within a 'systems approach', aware of the need to understand the interconnections between group functioning and the difficulties of individual members.

The group had met me weekly for two terms. Like some other groups, they then continued to meet on their own as a staff support group, inviting any other colleague to explore with them difficulties experienced with particular pupils, along the lines of the consultancy group. Two terms after its termination, interest was still growing among the rest of the staff, so that the formation of a second school group was being considered. 2 years later, members of the original group still came to the intermittent follow-up meetings arranged for their area in one of their feeder schools.

Preparing the ground for additional professional help

Let us, lastly, look at discussion of the kind of case where more specialised help is needed but where the school tries to 'battle on' or where permission for referral is withheld — often this refusal to grant permission for referral becomes more determined, the more the school tries to put its case, thereby possibly exacerbating a parent's 'need to prove that she (is) right and 'they' (are) wrong' (Dowling, 1985).

Len
Mrs. G., a teacher in another school-based group, had been valiantly trying to cope with Len, 5½ years old, and with the forceful grandmother who had brought him up, allowed his unmarried, tongue-tied mother no say in his upbringing and blamed the school for all his problems as listed by Mrs. G.

These were that Len was quite unable to concentrate, to co-ordinate his movements or even to use a pencil or to enjoy any activity, such as painting or sand play, which could improve his co-ordination. Never quiet or sitting still, he disturbed everybody very aggressively; he had not been taught how to eat without making a mess or when to go to the toilet, and so his food was everywhere and he smeared himself with excrement. He did, however, like doing sums and jigsaws, and Mrs. G. had always hoped that because of his brightness he would grow out of his difficulties, but this had not happened.

Discussing his symptoms, the group was helped to examine the probable confusions in this child's mind. His mother seemed too weak to claim him as hers, so that both she and the boy were treated as the grandmother's children. The daughter counted for nothing, and the grandson was always defended. Whatever he did was right in the grandmother's eyes; the child apparently ruled the household, and she placed the blame for his behaviour at school firmly in the school's court.

The situation seemed to be full of dissociations, and Len's needs too great for the school to meet without outside help, which the school now decided to ask for. In the meantime, the teacher's strategy of praise (which Len liked) and firmness (which he did not) could perhaps be combined, with both him and his grandmother. The group explored how this approach might be pursued with both, and especially with the grandmother, who was likely to resist the suggestion of child guidance help and would need the school's support (in spite of what they felt about her accusations!) to agree to take Len to the clinic — and to accept its advice.

The group returned to Len's case twice later that term. The grandmother's reaction against the idea of outside help had been even worse than expected; pounding her fist, she told the teacher and the headteacher that her own daughter had been 'messed about by the child guidance people' when she was small and that she would not 'let them now get hold of Len' — especially since her daughter was pregnant again and wanted to leave the home with Len to marry the baby's father.

The school, although unprepared for this flood of revelations, could now appreciate the grandmother's fears somewhat better. Further discussion enabled the teachers to be as supportive as possible, openly to appreciate her love for and attachment to Len and eventually to persuade her to take Len to the clinic. The grandmother warned them, however, that she would not 'open her mouth' there.

With these warnings, the group was encouraged to consider the grandmother's apparent fears and memories and was reminded of the many referrals for child guidance which do not survive the first appointment because of such fears and parents' reactions to being asked questions. This helped the school to prepare the clinic for this three-generation situation and the grandmother's anxieties. At the same time, the school endeavoured to give her consistent support as she continued her visits to the clinic, which Len then attended regularly. There his symptoms — some of which the teacher had not mentioned — were confirmed as signs of a severely distressed child, whom the school had seen as mainly a behaviour problem for them to cope with.

The school was enabled to give consistent support to the grandmother, whom they had formerly disliked for her hostility and her failure to appreciate their very real efforts to help Len. This helped him to receive and respond to the support which he needed. 4 months later, Mrs. G. reported that the grandmother had now, in her own way, become one of the school's most ardent supporters, turning up at every parents' meeting. Len was beginning to be less messy, and his grandmother was delighted that the clinic had called him 'intelligent'. However, she still rejected the clinic's advice to place him in a special day school, although she was willing to have a look at one. She also accepted that Len's mother wanted to leave home and start life with a husband and both Len and the new baby. This was to be arranged without interrupting Len's school life and his bonds with his grandmother.

This case discussion had served to overcome the initial hostility between home and school and their mutual blame for the child's difficulties, and had enabled the school to give sensitive support to the key parent figure. When the teachers could see the grandmother as a frightened woman and her anger at Len's teachers as part of her anxieties, they could also cease rejecting her unfair accusations and appreciate her desparate need to prove that she was doing her best for Len. The grandmother in her turn could then change her feelings for them, as both sides began to listen to each other. As Bowlby (1985) stresses, 'In all this work there is no outcome more to be hoped for than one in which the corrosion of mutual blame is banished and its place taken by mutual respect and goodwill. For it is only then that durable solutions can be expected.'

The exploration also illustrates how experienced, competent and caring teachers may yet be unaware of, or uncertain about, the significance of their observations. Not knowing which problems may be transitory and which indicate more deep-seated difficulties, the school had wished to shelter a bright child from the professional help he needed and thereby unwittingly colluded with the grandmother's own irrational wish to protect the child from the help that he could eventually be given. Once his need for it had been accepted, the school then also saw that they had to help to secure it, both by skilfully briefing the clinic about the grandmother's memories and fears regarding child guidance and by supporting the grandmother during a time which they were helped to recognise as extremely stressful to her. In this way the process of referral could be experienced positively by both sides, which workers engaged with both family and school (Lindsey, 1985) stress as a crucial aspect of school consultation.

Hitherto somewhat ambivalent in their communication with the clinic, the school felt that that link, too, was now much improved, as they were learning to approach them more as partners rather than defensively deferring to them as superior experts.

Summary

As we have seen, in none of these case discussions was there any attempt at issuing tips for teachers, or at telling others how to do their job and showing criticism of their methods. Instead, each case was jointly explored, with consultative guidance towards asking oneself the kinds of questions which might lead to better understanding of a child's exceptional needs and which might enable teachers to adapt their approach to the children in the course of their daily encounters. This took account of the teachers' needs for immediate support as well as of their need for information which would highlight issues and evoke the skills necessary to put insights and principles into practice beyond the immediate difficulty. The solutions which they attempted were their own and arose from their active involvement in the joint exploration of workable alternatives.

The questions regarding the children were concerned with:
- their actual behaviour and the responses that it generated: particular incidents, their antecedents and consequences as they involved the child in relation to others;
- whether these suggested anything about how the child saw himself and others in relation to him;
- whether there were attitudes ('I'm no good', 'everybody is against me', 'it's their fault' or 'I can only get attention if . . .') which could be understood in the context of what was known about his circumstances;
- whether these suggested anything about unmet needs and the new learning experiences which might help to meet them and which the teacher might be able to provide consistently over a stretch of time.

Questions about adapting their approach to the needs identified involved the teachers in considering curriculum content and learning activities, ways of getting in touch with the pupil without intrusion and mistiming — crucial at adolescence but important at any age — so that he would not feel constantly observed or 'understood' at the wrong moment. These included:
- knowing when and how to convey recognition of the pupil's

probable feelings about an incident, while setting him the limits that he might need;

- confronting the pupil constructively with his difficulty by building on his strengths, encouraging confidence and helping him to feel better about himself so that he can also see what is good in others;
- extending these experiences into the pupil's contacts with others at school and at home.

In this way, insight and skills were linked with the situation which had been presented as difficult, stressful and time consuming. What teachers found was that with unobtrusive interventions such as these they not only managed to be of more help to the children but also saved themselves stress and time in the classroom and that the time spent on case discussions was reducing the time that these pupils had hitherto 'made' them spend unproductively with them, which they could now use to good purpose.

The consultant took the role of catalyst (a poor analogy, since the consultant also changes in the process of joint exploration), supplementing the teachers' understanding with her own. This process requires one to use one's skills as a partner who can listen, to appreciate the teachers' perception of the difficulty in the context and constraints of their work setting and to utilise one's expertise in support of theirs. We shall examine in later chapters what is involved in applying support skills such as these.

3

Staff Support Groups: An Example of their Development in one Local Area

As we have seen, staff support and training groups can develop in very different settings. At secondary school level, Teresa's teacher was meeting only his own colleagues from within the school, all in middle management positions and thus potentially able to act as consultants to their colleagues, to convey to them in their turn the further expertise needed. In contrast, the secondary group which discussed John and Dipak was representative of the whole school and range of staff experience from senior pastoral care teacher to latest recruit to the profession. In the primary schools, Tony's, Don's, Michael's, Vic's, Dave's and Jeanie's teachers all belonged to groups representing two or more neighbouring schools, covering the whole age range of their pupils, and teachers of a wide range of experience (including secondary school intake staff, who found the discussion of younger pupils equally applicable to the secondary sector, as did the primary teachers with regard to the secondary staffs' contributions). Attendance could last from five weeks to one year, details being carefully negotiated with each school involved.

Detailed negotiation with each school and progress reports to other schools in the area with each new step in the development of support groups have been found to be essential by the evaluators of the SITE Project (cf. p. 2). In their evaluation report, Baker and Sikora (1982) (in association with J. P. Davies and A. T. Hider) give the following details on how groups of schools were first offered the teacher support service described in this book:

> '(Teacher support) work with a group of Project schools arose from the concern expressed by staff in several schools about what may be broadly defined as children with special needs within the ordinary school.

During their needs analysis, teachers had reported a worrying increase in the number of disruptive pupils from re-housed, multiproblem families who presented severe management problems in the classroom. The Project Co-ordinator approached a college-based consultant with previous training and experience in the education of children with special needs with a request to service some INSET activities for the schools concerned. Accordingly, the consultant met the heads of these schools as a group and subsequently the staff (without the heads) to outline the type of consultancy she considered would provide teachers with support and back-up to help them meet the needs of disturbed and disturbing children in their classes. After some discussion, agreement was reached for a series of weekly after-school meetings lasting one school year for the staff of 3 schools (1 First, 2 Middle) on one site and 2 schools (1 First and 1 Middle) on another. Later, one further First school joined the first group, increasing the number of participating schools on the site from 3 to 4.

The aims of the consultancy were to provide teachers with:
(a) some help with their immediate concerns, and
(b) a long-term developmental element of training in relation to underlying wider issues

which might also enable them to eventually build up or continue their own staff groups without the regular presence of a consultant. The consultancy setting, which was agreed during the negotiation between the provider and the schools, consisted of a structured joint exploration of the day-to-day difficulties presented by the children who gave them cause for special concern. During the weekly meetings of up to 12 teachers, a member of the group would present a 'case' with its most salient features, and the consultant and the other teachers would, in non-judgmental terms, ask for any further details about the child that they thought useful. This process of presentation, questioning, and discussion almost invariably brought into focus factors about the child not hitherto perceived as contributing to his behaviour pattern or the difficulties he/she was experiencing. These factors often related to the child's home or school setting, or turned attention to the quality of relationships with significant people in his present and/or past circumstances, if these were known. A guiding principle throughout these exchanges between teachers and the consultant was the autonomy of the teacher presenting the case, who would be left to decide what use to make of the ideas that emerged.

The Evaluator was able to attend 3 meetings of each of the groups meeting on the 2 school sites. It was evident that the information about disturbed and disturbing children that was pooled at these meetings led to a fresh perception of the pressures on children and of the difficulties for some in developing a positive self-concept because of their background circumstances. The discussion between the participants and the consultant's comment often opened up in the teacher's own mind, and in that of the others, some alternatives for action: in particular, how the child's self-image, for instance, might be 'extended into something more beneficial to him', linked with an exploration of 'therapeutic' classroom approaches designed to help both the child and the rest of the class.

As interest grew from the meetings, there was some disappointment in the schools that there could be only one group of 12 members for each site, which largely arose from the pressure of other work on the consultant. The latter had anticipated this particular difficulty during the original negotiation and had suggested that the support she hoped to offer should be extended to meet a wider range of teachers. Accordingly it had been agreed that the groups should contain:

(a) a mixture of self-selected staff from the different schools on the site serving the same community across the schools' age ranges

(b) that each school should have one or two core members willing to attend meetings throughout the year, and as many short-term members as would like to join the group, who would make way for new members at half-term or the end of terms.

The criteria for group membership were operated quite flexibly in that short-term members were able to return for follow-up of their cases, and additional teachers were accommodated for once-only case presentations. The core members gave both the groups the necessary continuity and stability . . .

A notable feature of the consultancy was the absence from all the meetings save those at the end of the year, of the head-teachers. This arose because the consultant believed that the presence of the headteachers, no matter how supportive the latter might be, would have altered the dynamic of the groups and made teachers less willing to externalise their problems. This was a view that all concerned, including the heads, who were initially somewhat disappointed at not being able to attend, came to accept. (For discussion of this issue, see pp. 114 f. (author's addition).)

Having staff from different schools on one site join together for these meetings had a number of positive effects. Firstly a wider range of teachers were often able to bring to light new dimensions in a pupil's life. For example, a child's past teacher(s) or colleagues who taught other members of the family were often able to contribute their knowledge of past upsets such as periods of abandonment by a parent, or other experiences of loss, separation, or rejection, and this helped to create fresh understanding in that child's present teacher. Secondly the membership of the groups promoted a strong increase in inter-school liaison on a number of issues, which in the case of disturbed and disturbing children, was typified by the example of a male member of staff from one of the Middle schools who was released to make regular visits to the feeder First school to work with children (mostly boys) who had no contact with a significant male figure either at home or at school. A further improvement in inter-school liaison occurred when members of staff from a transfer High school (which had also identified disturbed and disturbing children as an INSET need) joined the groups of First and Middle school teachers towards the end of the year.

By the end of the year, there were further outcomes from this consultancy. The Project Co-ordinator, after consultations with the LEA's Chief Inspector, arranged for the consultant to meet an invited audience of headteachers (and representatives) from the whole LEA to report on the consultancy that had taken place in the SITE Project schools and offer her services to other LEA schools in the following year. A number of the participating teachers from Project schools attended this meeting, and their comments and contribution to the discussion that followed lent an added authenticity to what the consultant had described. As a result of the meeting, a number of schools approached the consultant to service some further INSET, and meetings along the lines described above are currently taking place . . .

Comments on questionnaires and informal remarks addressed to the evaluator, together with the latter's own participant observation of some of these meetings, all pointed very strongly to the benefit for teachers in having their cases looked at dispassionately from the 'outside' with the consultant and other staff in the group. The following examples illustrate the gains that teachers felt they had achieved:

". . . confidence from knowing other teachers have as many doubts and problems as I do; and stimulation from the exchange of ideas; and I find I question my attitudes and actions far more than before."

"I am becoming a little more able to distance myself from isolated incidents and able to see how they relate to child's (or class's) problems. Practice in working out and trying strategies to help situations improve. Feeling that I am not alone in my position."

"A wider understanding of difficult children. A greater appreciation of the problems experienced by other teachers. An enlarged repertoire of approaches to try with problem children. A chance to get my own worries off my chest."

Teachers especially appreciated the atmosphere of supportive inter-dependence that the meetings established and in follow-up sessions were able at times to report 'dramatic improvements' in a child's response at school. While obviously welcoming any positive developments, the consultant was on these occasions at pains to point out the long-term nature of the strategy to help the child and emphasised that there could be no miracle cures. This was a perspective that the teachers themselves came increasingly to share:

"I came in the expectation of instant solutions — having to think things through was a nasty shock at first but now gives increasing satisfaction."

"These problems cannot be solved in a short space of time."

There were some within the LEA who considered that, at best, the consultant offered teachers in SITE Project schools techniques in the containment of children with behavioural or emotional difficulties, but the consultant's own stated aims and the format of the meetings do not lend much justification for this view. The emphasis of the consultancy was on helping the teacher to treat the child 'therapeutically' within the context and the matrix of relationships of the class, and in the light of discussion with other colleagues and (hopefully) parents. Observation of the meetings made it apparent that the consultant was equally concerned with underlying wider issues presented in an individual case and, above all, to help teachers to build for themselves a framework of analysis with which to consider the needs of other troubled and troublesome children and to find openings within their actual teaching to support their educational progress. There was also an obvious effort to preserve a balance between consultative input and joint exploration so that what teachers actually experienced could be highlighted by a few comments on, say, the dynamics of families or classroom groups and the effects of these on children with problems, so that the universal aspects of some cases could be discovered. It is not possible (here) to measure how far the consultancy enabled teachers in the event to build up their own staff groups, although there is evidence that core members have attempted to build support groups for existing and new staff during 1980–1 with only the occasional attendance by the outside consultant. (Follow-up meetings as late as 2 years after the ending of the weekly course showed that such groups had continued; cf. for instance p. 121.) (author's addition).)

Finally, evidence from questionnaires administered independently by the consultant and the evaluator indicated that the teachers' self-confidence and own self-monitoring skills developed and headteachers commented on a raised professionalism of staffroom discussion and a greater readiness of teachers to participate more actively at interprofessional clinic conferences.'

Examples from these and later groups given in Chapter 2 have shown how, regardless of the setting, consideration of a specific case enabled the consultant to promote among the staff, across departments and hierarchies, exploration of wider issues arising from it. The significance of seemingly baffling behaviour, the special needs that it may indicate, what responses to it might be appropriate and the need to understand one's own reaction to the needs expressed and the behaviour displayed are examples of the kind of issues which arose. We saw what a considerable capital of latent skills and personal resources such explorations can tap in teachers and make available for use in the classroom. Teachers, who were ambivalent about asking for help while expecting to be given advice, welcomed the chance of discovering and deciding for themselves how they might improve a pupil's situation. We saw how these processes developed and how their development in the core attenders (who chose to attend the group from first to last) benefitted short-term members and newcomers who learned from the questions which were being asked in the group on how to look for workable solutions. By extending their knowledge of the way in which situations and backgrounds can produce disturbance in a specific case, teachers were enabled to relax their hold on preconceived ideas about the child in question and about their own ineffectiveness with him. The group helped them to look with fresh eyes at the situation, to see it also from the pupil's point of view and to respond more adequately to the needs that his behaviour seemed to indicate. We saw how teachers became more objective, regained lost confidence in approaching pupils and were more able to make demands on them in a way which enabled the pupils to begin to meet them.

It is unclear how far the benefits accruing to the child are due to the teachers' attempts at better understanding of his needs or to the support which they themselves received in relation to their own concern about handling him. Both are suggested in the comments from eighty teachers who were questioned, in the course of detailed evaluations[1], about their experience of such school-based staff support groups, characteristically stressing that they found that:

- it was 'a relief to be allowed to have problems, to appreciate those of colleagues and to get practice in working out ways to improve situations for kids with difficulties';
- they 'no longer resented the time consumed by difficult pupils — I have come to like them!';
- 'to the extent to which one becomes effective with one's most difficult children, to that extent one is also a better teacher with the whole class';
- the skills which they possessed but did not always use could be effective with children with exceptional difficulties and could be applied in conjunction with new skills learnt;
- they felt more confident in their relationships with pupils' parents;
- they had developed a better partnership with colleagues from their own and feeder schools and, in some instances, with those from outside support services ('. . . Discussions within the group and suggestions from (the consultant) led me to feel more confident that I could do something to help these children. In addition, I was more confident in getting in touch with and dealing with outside agencies in order to help the children, e.g. the child guidance clinic, welfare workers, parents, the school psychologist').

As a result of progress report meetings to invited audiences of headteachers and representatives such as that referred to in the above account (pp. 48 ff.) and similar meetings since (now also taking the form of progress reports to individual schools) more schools requested to start or join support groups, and these were offered lasting from one to three terms in consecutive years. Headteachers, promoting the idea of such support work at senior and middle management level, suggested that a consultancy group be formed for the headteachers themselves, with the following aims:

(a) to discuss children's special needs in classroom and school and to explore how schools can help to meet them;
(b) to examine ways, similar to those found effective in the staff support and training groups, in which staff may be helped by senior staff to extend their skills with such pupils.

Such a group of headteachers was then started, to meet weekly for one term in the first instance. The group was extended by unanimous request to the full academic year and eventually ran for two years, continuing after that, like a number of other groups, with only intermittent attendance by or contact with the consultant.

Developments such as these offer valuable pointers for the advancement of support work with colleagues and the training of specially qualified members of staff for such work by other professionals (an opportunity which we shall examine in Part III). They highlight the extent of the need for such support and show how readily schools accept it when its remit has been clarified and use is made of the communication channels open to inform schools about it. They emphasise how support of this kind ought to be concerned with any teacher and with any child's special needs. It clearly need not be, nor should it be, confined to the more extreme cases which are referred elsewhere for specialised treatment by outside agencies or to those children who are helped through school-based direct behavioural and psychotherapeutic counselling individual or group methods. What is demonstrated is that some of the principles and practices with which those with special expertise manage to meet children's special needs can be systematically conveyed to the teachers and that teachers are interested in knowing more about them. Teachers are concerned about the difference between what they sense ought to be done in response to children's special needs and their actual reaction to them. They are, as these developments show, ready to accept the kind of support which makes such knowledge and skill available to them, reduces the discrepancy, taps and maximises their own resources and so helps them to find for themselves solutions for these children, as part of the pursuit of their professional goals.

As has been shown, there are powerful arguments in favour of extending to all teachers some of the expertise available both in the schools' pastoral care and special needs support systems and in the whole network of child guidance and care services and of making such support an accepted part of their remit. Since the seminal recommendations of the Warnock (1978) Report that LEAs should move towards more effective support for the class teacher — reinforced six years later by the Advisory Committee on the Supply and Education of Teachers (ACSET, 1984) — with regard to the special needs facing him daily, increasing attention has been paid by many local authorities to the restructuring of their resources towards this end (Gipps and Goldstein, 1984). Extra staff have been recruited to cope with the additional psychological demands arising from the 1981 Education (Special Needs) Act, and grants have been allocated nationally for new in-service courses for that purpose. As we have seen, such courses can be offered in the schools by professionals with special expertise in the field to a maximum number of teachers (cf. Part III for practicalities). They can overcome the poverty of training opportunities in ordinary schools and the arbitrariness seen as inherent in choosing only some teachers to send away on courses (Mittler, 1984), as the school-based course can be structured as a normal institutional in-service feature. Evidence shows that pressure of time on such experts and on classroom teachers need not be an obstacle to wider deployment of staff expertise. Early consultation in a group setting has been shown to decrease the pressures on both groups of professionals, which arise on the one hand, from belated or inappropriate referrals with long waiting lists as a result or, on the other, having to teach children whose needs one does not fully understand. As has been pointed out (Wolff, 1969; Daines *et al*, 1981), the question is not one of extra time but of skill and flexibility in the use of expertise. Each professional willing to share his understanding with groups of other professionals will have his own way of using it. To do so effectively, however, requires special inter-professional skills, based on an understanding of the work setting in which they are to be exercised. It is to these 'aspects of the landscape' of teacher support work that we now turn.

Note
Baker and Sikora (1982) and Hider (1981) evaluated the groups which formed part of the DES-funded SITE Project (1978–81). This was continued by Hanko (1982) under the auspices of the University of London Institute of Education as work approved for the Associateship of the Institute. The settings evaluated ranged from one- to three-term groups and comprised:
(a) inter-school groups with core and short-term membership across the range of career experience;
(b) inter-school membership with homogeneous status or experience (headteachers or middle management staff only; teachers in their second year of teaching);
(c) intra-school membership across one school's departmental boundaries and managerial hierarchy from first appointments to senior management;
(d) intra-school membership drawn from middle management positions.

PART II
A Framework for Teacher Support

4

Approaches to Treatment and Consultation

Approaches to treatment

Teachers looking for support in dealing with children's emotional and behavioural difficulties from their specialist colleagues on the school staff or the outside support services may find that these base their practice on different theoretical assumptions. All of them would be able to provide useful support. Unfortunately, adherents of the psychodynamic and behaviouristic theories of personality development may both disparage each other's theory and the method derived from it and claim their own base as uniquely effective. Kolvin *et al* (1982), who compared and evaluated these direct approaches to children, found their competing claims largely irrelevant. Significant improvements appeared with both approaches, and what differences there were in improvement during treatment had disappeared by the time of their final follow-up.

It is doubtful whether those who advocate either model exclusively and focus entirely either on symptoms or on causes offer the practitioner in the classroom the full perspective of what he could achieve. We saw how, in our groups, teachers were helped to deal with the children's difficulties within the context in which they occur. They were encouraged to approach symptoms directly as well as to examine what might be wrong in the whole situation for the child, how that situation might be improved and how they could help the child to cope with it through better understanding. Jeanie's teacher (pp. 33–35), for instance, used the technique of ignoring the irritating behaviour by which the child was seeking the attention that she craved but of rewarding her with attention whenever she was helpful less obtrusively (a behavioural technique). She also used her understanding of the child's motivation by talking to her about what makes people accept and reject help and about the feelings that we can all have about rebuffs and how we can deal with them, thus helping her to understand herself better. This was a behavioural approach but incorporated psychodynamic understanding. It must be distinguished from the use of behavioural methods without attempting to understand what needs the behaviour may express. Although mere reaction to surface behaviour might bring 'surface managerial success' (cf. Kounin *et al*, 1965), it might not meet the underlying need in cases such as these or might even *increase* it, even if the symptoms can be made to disappear. Others (e.g. Lim and Bottomley, 1983; Wilson and Evans, 1980; Laslett, 1982) have advocated combining forms of treatment and have described in detail the beneficial results of such a flexible combination of methods, in contrast with those who pigeon-hole practices, rejecting those which they perceive as belonging to rival schools, and 'cling to their separate claims'.

Such claims are often combined with a stereotyped misconception of 'the other side'. Some followers of a psychodynamic approach seem to perceive as behaviour therapy only its most radical Skinnerian brand of automatic conditioning. They are apparently unaware that some leading advocates of behavioural methods also reject this, stress their roots in social learning and cognitive psychologies and themselves deprecate some of their colleagues' misapplications as 'mindless technology' (Berger, 1979a, 1979b). The psychodynamic school accuses behaviourists of over-simplifying complex problems, while the behaviourists consider simplification unavoidable, or even a scientific virtue, believing that 'needs are best met by ignoring the complexities' (Yule, 1974).

Behaviourists, on their side, may dismiss psychodynamic attempts at understanding difficult behaviour as a useless search for causes in a distant past (Ainscow and Tweddle, 1979) which cannot be changed. They ignore the fact that perception of the past can be modified by new perspectives and experiences and that assumptions based on past experiences can be challenged by new learning experiences. They may also think that it is useless to speculate about happenings in the child's family and to consider the child's past and his family experiences, since both are beyond the teacher's control (emphasising control rather than influence). It is also suggested that, if teachers take such factors into consideration, they may see them as excuses for difficult behaviour ('poor Tom, he has such a difficult home'), do nothing to change it and allow themselves to be distracted from what they can control in the classroom in furtherance of the child's progress.

Most rejective polarisations — if they are not just parodies — can highlight, however, the potential hazards of mindless misapplications, such as do sometimes occur. We should therefore not assume that the critics are simply misinformed or concerned merely to establish the superiority of their own standpoint. Clearly 'insight' alone, if used (or abused) simply as an excuse for inaction, would be as uneducational as the mere manipulation of surface behaviour.

The two approaches themselves, when properly applied, seem to be increasingly complementary. It is a tenet of behavioural theory that behaviour is shaped by the antecedents which evoke it and the consequences which maintain it. Attention should therefore focus on the child's actual behaviour, its antecedents and spin-offs, i.e. how undesirable behaviour is reinforced by its consequences. Such reinforcement (e.g. the negative attention which reinforces the attention-seeker's bad behaviour) should therefore be avoided, and the desired forms of behaviour systematically encouraged and rewarded whenever they occur (positive reinforcement). What is advocated is to teach the child a repertoire of new skills 'without speculation about links between earlier experiences and current problems', to concentrate on the special environment and to manipulate its features. A token economy system (awarding and withholding tokens in accordance with the behaviour displayed) is one form of such manipulation.

Yet behaviourists are also concerned with the child's history and his family situation and background, since behaviour is socially learned and influenced by private experience, by what we 'make' of the events of our lives, by how we perceive, think and feel about them and by how we learn to own experiences as ours. Behaviourists also now no longer disregard the relationship between them and the child as irrelevant to the success of the technique, which was previously seen as 'therapist proof'. They now consider 'what the client thinks about and feels about the therapist and the approach, and what the therapist thinks and feels about the client . . . to be important conditions' (Berger, 1979), at least as 'motivating properties' for the technique to become effective.

It is the psychodynamic view that patterns of early experience affect later ones and that later difficulties tend to find their antecedents in significant earlier experiences in the family, which can establish expectations and assumptions about later relationships and the role adopted in them. Treatment rests on the assumption that such expectations and responses can be superseded by new and specially structured learning experiences (see for instance Teresa's case (pp. 19–22)). It is not always necessary to delve into a child's past to understand his behaviour, since the behaviour itself can tell us something about how he sees himself, what he has come to expect others to do to him and how he may interpret what we do accordingly. It follows that one can learn to discriminate and to perceive the difference between new experiences in the present and the stereotyped assumptions based on the past. It is believed that people are helped to cope with current problems if their feelings and anxieties are shared and understood. As has been shown in the case of teachers (Chandler, 1980), they may be unable to solve home problems but 'can go a long way towards alleviating them if they recognise that they exist'.

Increasing acceptance by behaviourists of the importance of such intangibles as present and past relationships and experiences and what is felt about them, and the psychodynamic focus on here-and-now behaviour dynamics, will make things easier for the classroom teacher, who does not see why only a child's outward behaviour, or only what he has come to feel about his world, should be considered. As we saw, teachers in the consultancy groups seemed to see no contradiction in considering and trying to modify both, with differing emphases according to the difficulties displayed. Their attention was directed to the child's whole situation and its disturbing features. The aim was always to extend experience beyond the probable influence of past experiences and reaction patterns and, mindful of such possible influences on present behaviour and on what it seemed to express, to provide opportunities to experience new situations and to learn alternative ways of interacting. The teachers' here-and-now problem-oriented approach to behavioural and learning difficulties also included considering possible influences and implied that teachers had to be able to learn *from* the child. (One of Warnock's (1982) reservations about an exclusive behaviour modification approach is that 'it supposes that the teacher always knows best'.) They helped the child to understand himself and his behaviour without invading his privacy, as we saw for instance with Tony (pp. 14–18). They used both psychodynamic and behaviour-oriented premises that, on the one hand, problematic behaviour (unless biophysically determined) expresses something for the child, arising from unmet need and expectations rooted in the past and that, on the other hand, something in the present situation coincides with those expectations and helps to activate or maintain that behaviour. By establishing new learning experiences within a consistently constructive educational relationship, teachers could more fully realise the therapeutic elements in educational procedures, in relation to a child's special needs, while respecting his privacy. (This distinguishes it from other psychodynamic approaches such as counselling, psychotherapy or family therapy.) This way of helping children was not only well within a teacher's scope but, as has been argued (Elliott, 1982), is also clearly within the educational mandate. In contrast, where behavioural techniques remain purely manipulative, they may, unless expertly applied, produce short-lived changes specific to the situation. (For instance, one teacher using the technique found a pupil improving his classroom behaviour in accordance with the teacher's rewards but then received complaints from the mother that she could not get him to do anything now without first promising a reward.) Such behavioural techniques may lead to a mere conformism in the child or to repetitive and arid teaching and may lack the cognitive element required for a legitimate part of the educational process.

The concept of consultation and its practice in schools

While there are as many interpretations of the term consultation as there are contexts in which it is useful 'to consider jointly' and 'to take counsel', (cf. Eraut's (1977) typology of roles of expert, resource provider, promoter, career agent, link agent, evaluator, legitimator, ideas man, process helper, counsellor and change agent) it has become a well-defined concept in the mental health context.

As has been demonstrated, consultation is here seen not as a process in which a professional acts as a 'problem-solving expert who can provide (others with a) solution or a set of . . . alternative courses of action' but as a 'non-directive interventionist (with three primary tasks: 'to generate valid information . . .; to maintain the client's autonomy by enabling him to make free and informed choices about the nature of the intervention; and to enable a high degree of commitment . . . to its implementation . . . on the part of the client' (Bell, 1979) (cf. Bell's exposition of the two main types of consultants in accordance with Argyris' (1970) analysis). This requires him to generate an atmosphere in which consultant and consultees can work together as professionals with equal but differing expertise, engaged in a process of joint exploration which seeks to develop the consultees' professional understanding and skills concerning a third party (such as the pupils). The consultant supplements the consultees' expertise with his own, thereby helping to highlight the issues underlying the case to be explored and enabling the consultees to arrive at new solutions. The atmosphere generated is that of what Bion (1961) calls a 'work group', functioning openly in relation to an agreed task, unimpeded as far as possible by hidden preoccupations ('hidden agendas') with leadership and other issues (Bion's 'basic assumptions') through which groups may seek to avoid tackling the task (note for instance Dipak's case and discussion (pp. 39–43).

The consultant as informed facilitator — not didactic instructor — is thus no judge, assessor or supervisor of the consultee's performance, nor has he a mandate for personal therapy or counselling. He must therefore not allow the discussion to focus on personal problems which may influence a consultee's handling of the case (as we saw, these may nevertheless be relieved indirectly as the case is being discussed). Consultation based on case discussions also differs from the traditional case conference. It is understood as a regular series of meetings between consultees and consultant, who has not himself met the child to be discussed or, if he has, has less knowledge of the child than the consultees. In contrast, case conferences are *ad hoc* meetings for reports and discussion between all the professionals in contact with a case.

Whether the consultant comes to the school from outside or is already on the staff as a special needs support or pastoral care teacher, all the considerations outlined apply to the consultancy model that he chooses to extend the teachers' understanding of children's behaviour, its effects and treatment and the significance of the teachers' part in dealing with it.

Followers of both behavioural and psychodynamic approaches agree that teachers can be helped to deal with problem behaviour which interferes with their teaching and the child's ability to learn. They differ, however, on whether it is best to give direct advice and prescription, the view held in the former approach or, as is the aim of the latter approach, to help teachers to see for themselves how the situation may be contributing to the child's difficulties and to discover how to improve it by educational means. Consultants of this type consider it important for teachers to make their own decisions as autonomous professionals, in the light of increased understanding and better use of related skills which they already possess and are developing further.

Behavioural practitioners offer their own techniques of assessment and intervention (cf. Ellis 1985) which teachers can learn without much difficulty, for instance by direct training in how to spot children 'being good' and how to use positive reinforcement effectively. They collaborate with the teacher, for example through the use of check-lists, during the implementation of the technique recommended.

They also use techniques of behavioural reinforcement with the teachers themselves, praising them for successful application of the method. The approach is available in teaching packages such as Behavioural Approach to Teaching Package (BATPACK), which is offered by a research project funded by the Schools Council (Wheldall, 1982), or has been described in one local authority's Special Needs Action Programme (SNAP) (Muncey and Ainscow, 1983). As Galloway (1985) reminds us, however, integration of children with exceptional needs may be inhibited by the specialised nature of a behavioural objectives programme.

While consultation based on psychodynamic principles similarly focuses attention on the child's behaviour and situation, it also takes into account the teacher's perception of the difficulty and its effects on him, such as erosion of confidence or loss of objectivity. It helps him to deal with these effects, as was illustrated in the case studies. This model of consultancy does not prescribe what the teacher should do but highlights the issues — in accordance with the non-directive interventionist role — in an enabling way which points towards workable alternatives. The teacher is left to decide how to use his own extended understanding and skills with the child in question and ultimately in other problematic situations.

These crucial aspects of the educational process suggest the Caplan model of consultation (Caplan, 1970; Plog and Ahmed, 1977; Irvine, 1979; Conoley, 1981) as particularly appropriate in the educational context since it focuses on maximising the teachers' own resources to deal more effectively with a pupil who presents them with problems. In contrast with the Balint (1957) model which is based on similar premises but deals directly with the worker–client relationship, the Caplan model does so only indirectly, as has already been elaborated. The consultee may have insufficient knowledge or understanding in relation to the particular case and therefore may not use his skills appropriately, as well as needing confidence and objectivity to be restored. Although lack of objectivity may be due to a problem in the teacher's situation which is reflected in the child's problem, this is never explicitly mentioned, since the consultant has no sanction for therapy. However, by reducing the teacher's anxiety about the child's problem and helping him to understand it better and to think out possible solutions, the consultant will disentangle it from the teacher's own anxiety and may thus indirectly help to relieve it. We have seen that this enabled the teachers to take a fresh look at the situation and to discover ways of improving it.

The Caplan model is thus in accord with what is now seen as

constituting effective in-service provision (cf. p. 2 ff.) and studies of organisational structures (Argyris, 1963, 1982) which emphasise that their key workers need to perceive themselves as responsible decision-makers entitled to find their own professionally acceptable solutions to the problems they encounter. However, teachers frequently 'collectivise' or 'privatise' their professional problems — to use Lacey's (1977) terms — by blaming the establishment or the pupils for them or by keeping them dark, fearing that problems are signs of personal ineptitude. Teachers agree, in discussion, that these 'solutions' do not advance their professional task and also that it is notoriously difficult to use advice which seems to imply criticism of their methods.

The Caplan model forestalls this, as it provides a supportive structure which can enable teachers to accept responsibility for finding workable solutions to many of their difficulties with pupils and to experience heightened professionalism in consequence. The model also allows them to use those approaches which best suit their way of working, to examine these in relation to the educational task and to gain self-understanding in the educational context without actual exposure. This cognitive element of the model, demonstrable in the consultancy setting, enables teachers to transfer the understanding and skills gained to other children apart from the one discussed. This again makes the method particularly suitable for teachers in view of their role and their institutional setting and reinforces and extends those aspects — defining problems and helping others to deal with them — which good pastoral teachers already see as their function.

Few consultants will adopt any one model exclusively, and there is considerable overlap between models. In our case, the approach exemplified in the case discussions is based on the Caplan model of jointly focusing on current work problems. It also contains a *training element*, in that it broadens the discussions of specific cases by highlighting issues in such a way that the whole group — whether or not other members know the child — learn a problem-solving approach which they can apply to meeting future problems and needs as they may arise (cf. Wall (1977, 1979), for the importance of this aspect of support).

No matter which model a consultant adapts to his or her own way of working, he/she will find it useful to note the successes and difficulties reported by others. For instance, Kolvin *et al* (1982) combined the role of outside consultant with that of parent counsellor and found that this gave rise to certain difficulties (for examples of doing so successfully, cf. Taylor (1982, 1985) (cf. also p. 96), Dowling and Osborne's (1985) joint systems approach) and Ellis (1985). They also seem not to have obtained provision for regular group discussions, so that the consultant could only meet the teachers in their individual free moments. This sometimes meant talking separately to as many as 16 teachers about the same children. Furthermore this arrangement focused discussion exclusively on a specific case without opportunities for teachers to consider its wider relevance. Unsurprisingly, as stressed by one reviewer (Wolff, 1983), teacher consultation without regular group discussion was not as effective as it might otherwise have been. (cf. also Ellis (1985)).

Time pressures were also part of the difficulties noted by Daines *et al* (1981) in their study of a child guidance consultation service. The service was found to be successful in that it did lead to more appropriate referrals to the clinic (one of the aims behind the clinic's support service). Meetings, however, arranged during lunchtimes lasted only from ½ hour to 1 hour and always felt rushed. Teachers drifted in and out because of conflicting commitments, and themselves saw this as counterproductive to thoughtful discussions — as must have been the case with the number of pupils (ranging from four to fifteen cases) discussed at any one meeting. Attendance fluctuated according to the pupils to be discussed, since tutors tended to attend only for 'their own' cases and to lose interest when other children were discussed, unaware that the discussion of each case could lead to insights for everyone. Actual classroom teachers attended only very occasionally and were therefore inclined to be daunted by the hierarchically top-heavy membership of the group. Size, too, prevented some from contributing.

The clinic staff attended as a team and therefore had to cope with their own hierarchy. The observers were impressed by the good relationship and trust which had developed between the clinic and the schools, but they felt that the team missed opportunities of alleviating the teachers' anxieties and work-related pressures by making their understanding explicit. They seemed to aim mainly to help the child to adapt to the school system, without much consideration of his interaction with other children and teachers and with the school itself. They also seemed to have missed opportunities of giving recognition and showing appreciation of the teachers' work and thus of encouraging further development of their skills — inhibited perhaps by fears of transgressing boundaries but thereby falling short of the Caplan model in these respects.

In spite of these difficulties, schools and clinic had achieved a viable on-going consultation system which had led to better communication between both institutions and a better service. As the observers stress, even more could have been achieved with explicit clarification of purpose and structure, established from the outset and constantly renewed as members change. We shall examine in Part III what this entails for both 'in-house' and outside consultants.

5
The Meetings: Purposes and Foci

Whatever a school's work setting, the rationale of the sessions described in Part I was, as we saw, to build on the teachers' experience and on their knowledge of the learning process, of child development and of human behaviour, while perceiving such knowledge as capable of supplementation by outside professionals or specially appointed members of staff with additional experience or special understanding of exceptional needs. As was shown, they need not themselves have met the child discussed or, if on the staff, may not know him well as does the teacher who presents his case. The process of joint exploration with such a qualified colleague is utilised to enable teachers to redirect their perceptions and to answer for themselves the questions raised in the exploration rather than having them answered for them. Through examining the underlying issues in this way, they are more likely to see what may be wrong in the situation for a child and how they might make better use of their own skills and educational means to improve that situation and to help the child to cope, as they realise more fully the therapeutic side of educational methods and relationships. They may then see how much more they can do as teachers faced with the special needs of the whole range of children. They may come to realise that even 'maladjustment' is not a qualitatively distinct condition necessarily to be treated by experts and that their own professional skills may be relevant also and, especially, in the face of emotional, behavioural and learning difficulties.

In each session, with the focus on a specific child, knowledge and skills were shared which might help the teacher to understand and deal with that case better, and the whole group with similar ones. *Knowledge* which would help to restore *objectivity* about the situation and *skills* which would heighten the teacher's *confidence* with regard to the task were shared, so that the teachers were able to muster their resources and to use them more effectively in support of the child's progress.

Knowledge was shared with regard to:

(a) the child, concerning how emotional, behaviour and learning difficulties develop (disturbance-producing experiences);
(b) the whole classroom group in relation to the child — as part of the dynamics of groups with regard to individual differences (disturbing behaviour may have a function for the group who could instead be helped to support his learning);
(c) managing the teacher–pupil interaction in the face of special needs and behaviour difficulties;
(d) the therapeutic potential in the day-to-day curriculum.

The skills which were shared related to:

(a) gauging the needs of a specific case from the behaviour displayed;
(b) making special bridging efforts to reach the child's 'teachable self';
(c) providing a consistent setting of new learning experiences likely to meet the needs gauged;
(d) involving, if possible, the child's parents and, if necessary, colleagues (fellow-teachers and members of other professions) as genuine partners.

Consistent attention to the issues underlying the specific case ensured that the whole group remained involved regardless of whether or not they knew the child discussed at any one session, and this helped the development of problem-solving skills for use in other cases. We must now see what this involved in detail.

Sharing knowledge

As we have seen, the consultant offers information as required for the understanding of the case under discussion beyond the behaviour displayed, to assist the discovery of ways of appropriate management. Its relevance must be clear, and it must be offered in a way which does not suggest that the consultant sees himself as sole expert and which will not further undermine the teacher's confidence, already likely to be dented by the difficulty of the case.

Secondly, it is clearly crucial — whether the consultant is a specially trained member of staff or an expert from outside — that the teachers are respected as autonomous professionals; thus the sharing of knowledge must reflect the consultancy principle of joint exploration between partners who contribute their equal but different expertise. The consultant's contribution is one among others. He helps to highlight the issues, balancing his input with joint exploration and heightening the teachers' sense of autonomy by encouraging them to draw on their latent resources and enabling them to approach their task with fresh understanding and confidence. This is at the same time an example of how the teacher might approach the pupil.

The consultant thus builds on the teacher's own professional knowledge which as a pastoral or counselling colleague he shares and which as an outside consultant he needs to make clear that he appreciates. Some of this may have become dated, outdated or inadequate; some of it may have become cliché ridden and thereby arid, such as the 'self-fulfilling prophecy' or pseudo-explanations such as the 'broken home' and the 'one-parent family'.

As we saw in the case discussions, the information needed related to three main areas: the child 'out there', with his experiences which governed his reaction to situations; the child and his group of co-learners; the teacher in interaction with them.

(i) About the child

The child 'out there' may disappoint or affront teachers by rebuffing their best-intentioned efforts to help him to learn; the child may perplex them by going out of his way to make himself disliked; the child may make them feel useless because he won't try and is convinced that he can't do what they require. In these and other ways the child invites and habitually receives the rejecting or despairing response which confirms his own expectations. This is in accordance with what is known about those 'aspects of perceptual distortion, inappropriate emotion and manipulative action (which tend to transform the present person and the present situation into the image and likeness of an earlier person and a past situation' (Irvine, 1979). As teachers deepen their understanding of such patterns, they find it increasingly possible to resist such attempts, to break out of the vicious circle in which they have been trapped and to help the child to find more fruitful ways of relating and to tackle his work with more hope.

The child's behaviour becomes understandable through applying information on how behaviour patterns are learned and how self-concepts are shaped to what is known of his circumstances and history. The group can then consider what approaches teachers can use to enable a child to establish different relationships with teachers and classmates, which can help to supersede his erroneous ideas about himself as hopeless, unacceptable and unworthy or about others as hostile, rejecting and indifferent.

Teachers found it useful to consider how children may try to deal with family anxieties in school, how they may be differently affected at different stages of development by what precedes and follows the break-up of a home, how siblings from seemingly intact families can confront their teachers with puzzling behaviour differences — which affect their learning — according to the different family roles imposed on them, how bereaved parents may hinder a child from expressing his own grief, how an abandoned parent may try to discredit the one who has left, unaware of the hazards for a child not allowed to think well of both his parents, and how this too may affect him at school.

As the underlying issues became clearer, no decisions were made for the teachers by providing clinical diagnoses or advice on treatment, nor was it suggested that they should tackle complex family relationships or strive to obtain such intimate knowledge beyond what parents willingly divulge. The teachers, on their own account, became more attentive to the clues available by discussing the implications of the issues, and this also helped them to respond more appropriately to the children's transient or long-term needs. We have seen how teachers learned to pay more attention to the situation in which a child began to behave in problematic ways and to his response to the measures taken to 'correct' this, and what these may represent to him. By viewing behaviour symptoms as part of a pattern of possible anxieties and defences against them, symptoms began to indicate the probable nature of the difficulty and of the kinds of learning experience which might help a child to cope more effectively, in mutually satisfying and less crippling relationships.

(ii) About the classroom group

The child's group of co-learners, however, may not wish him to change — a frequent cause of frustration for teachers, when their sensitive handling of an individual child is brought to nothing by the reactions of the group, which may oppose his improvement. Undercurrents in the classroom, if merely controlled from the top or if left to themselves, can, as every teacher knows, block his every effort with one child whose peers may not 'allow' him to transcend his group role of trouble-maker, victim, clown or scapegoat. One can then examine how the learning experiences which teachers may design for an individual pupil need to take into account the whole class for the child's sake as much as for the personal and social education of the others; this is as important as helping any particular child to see others in a new light. The pressures which operate in classroom groups, however, are frequently regarded by teachers as being 'in the nature of things', which they think they can do little to change other than by suppressing their worst features.

Teachers therefore found it useful to examine how groups, because of tensions in the group as a whole, can make use of particular individuals to express the group's needs and to understand the collusive roles played by other children in reinforcing individual behaviour difficulties. Having a class in hysterics at his deliberate antics may represent success for the class clown, staving off his fear that he might otherwise arouse their derision. Autobiographical accounts testify how behind children's many other 'nasty manoeuvres . . . (may lie) the hidden fear that (they themselves) might at any moment fall from favour and become the object of contempt' (James, 1980). An understanding of group theory has helped teachers to see that the class clown may also be expressing something on behalf of the group and that other group roles may be similarly assigned — the rebel, the provocateur, the disrupter, the scapegoat and similar victims, the dunce, the swot and the conciliator. Each role expresses needs or desires for the other members of the group and is carried by the one for whom they are most urgent or least controllable, who is thus singled out to play the role and to suffer the restrictions that it can impose on his development as a whole person. As we saw in Don's and Martin's case (p. 23ff.), if a child is then helped to overcome such role restriction — a restriction with which Mrs. B. found she had colluded — or, if the bearer of such a role is absent or leaves, it may come to be adopted by another pupil. Most teachers have found this when rash enough to feel relief at the absence of a harassing child.

Better understanding of group processes and of the teacher's part in those processes can help them to consider what a classroom group may see as its purposes. Whether the purpose is co-operation with a teacher whom they perceive to be on their side, or rejection of another who appears to reject them, the group will collude with those of its members willing to express those wishes. Alerting teachers to these possibilities has enabled them to try out alternative methods of group management, to avoid collusion with a group's irrational needs, and instead activate the group's potential in support of each child's learning.

At the same time, information about the possible links between the needs of individuals and the dynamics of groups has helped teachers not to feel personally hurt, affronted, disappointed or surprised at unexpected undercurrents in overtly co-operative groups or individuals and to realise the potential for co-operation in those who are overtly hostile. It has helped them to steer these undercurrents towards more constructive support, even for the group's most vulnerable members.

To achieve this, teachers must know and remember how to foster the unifying forces in groups — feelings of belonging, self-esteem, constructive purpose, security in the absence of threat — and to reduce divisive tensions, such as rivalrous dependence on the teacher or on powerful group members, which may activate resentments and fears. Teachers can then see for themselves how their ways of managing a class, as well as ordinary curriculum content, can provide learning experiences (as we shall examine in detail in a later section) to further the children's understanding of themselves and the world around them and to apply this in their relationships with each other.

If teachers can consider, in specific cases, that reparative forces may be latent in overtly opposed groups and individuals, they can also examine whether the climate of their institution influences their own readiness to work with or to oppose such forces as they exercise their authority. They can learn from such examples as Jimmy Boyle's (1977) ('Scotland's most violent man') account of his schooldays, when he felt, at ten years old, that the teachers who punished his violence so severely did not really want him to be less so, or as the 'relevant incident' used to highlight Dave's (p. 30) and other cases. These remind teachers of the choice which they may forget that they have — either to ignore this reparative potential and to leave it untapped, so that even the offenders remain unaware of it, or to learn to find and uncover it and to become able to 'confirm' the group and the pupil accordingly.

(iii) About the teacher–pupil interaction

Teachers can then see that the way in which we respond to children's needs and difficulties depends not only on our knowledge about children and the groups in which they move but also on how well we understand ourselves and our reactions to the range of special needs, especially if displayed in disturbing or abnormal behaviour. It is well known that, although we may be trained as professionals, we may continue to respond to the many difficulties that we encounter, not as professionals, but with our 'untutored selves' (Kahn and Wright, 1980). Not to do so requires self-awareness and, for teachers, an understanding of the personal aspects which may influence relationships between teachers and learners. The case discussions illustrated two main features of the learning process in consultancy support groups: that members should develop sufficient understanding of what is 'out there' in the object of the investigation and that they should note and deal for themselves with what assumes personal significance for them. As has already been stressed (cf. Chapter 4) and demonstrated (e.g. in Dave's case discussion (p. 30)), the absence of a mandate for taking up personal references in consultancy — which is not psychotherapy — requires that such self-understanding should be furthered only through reference to what is universal in such relationships, and without reference to individuals.

We saw in John's case (pp. 36–39) how this may be done. There, the group examined how a pupil's bad feelings about himself may be aggressively projected onto 'convenient' teachers. It briefly considered the links between the way in which our own aggressions had been handled when we were children and the demands that we may later make on others and thus influence how convenient a target we become for their aggression. If this is understood, teachers become aware of how a whole range of anxieties relate to what we feel about success, failure and inadequacy and to the demands that we make on ourselves and others. This can help teachers to handle and even to forestall those battles with pupils in which both sides feel persecuted and picked on by the other and in which the defensive provocations of one side become 'evidence' of the other's badness. When this was put as generally valid — i.e. not concerning just one teacher — teachers themselves saw how one may be tempted to 'deal with' a pupil so as to stop his expressing and challenging one's own unacknowledged doubts about one's competence. They could also see that acceptance of doubts and difficulties, far from reflecting negatively on their competence, could in fact add to it and that, if they understood the possibility of such mutual 'projective identifications', they found it easier to survive their impact. By not retaliating, they could help a pupil with his feelings, gently reflecting them back to the pupil and acknowledging that he will have reasons for them, and could help him to see that, even if one has such reasons, one does not have to act them out on others. We saw how this had helped, for instance, Tony (pp. 14–18) and Vic (pp. 27–29).

To apply insights such as these requires teachers to try to understand what they themselves are made to feel by their pupils and then to use this self-understanding to gain access to the pupil's related problems, to his experience and eventually to his 'teachable self'.

What Oakeshott (1973a) called discovering the pupil's 'conflict-free areas' needs to be preceded by widening one's own. Both are aided in the consultancy process, without having to bring any teacher's actual feelings into the discussion.

As we have seen, teachers enjoy the full involvement in the sharing of knowledge which arises if the consultant maintains a balance between contributing his expertise and eliciting theirs. In different sessions, this balance may be tilted one way or the other, as we saw in the case study sequences. The consultant can restore the balance if he too asks for help and clarification and admits that he lacks the knowledge which others in the group possess — such as their knowledge of the children that he may not know or, in the case of an outside consultant, matters of institutional organisation which he has not himself experienced. Caplan (1970) finds that the consultant's expertise is best offered by 'asking answerable questions' to generate insight but without undermining the group members' confidence which may have been damaged by their failure to solve the problem. If one includes oneself among those who might not at once have understood what was happening ('most children could react in this way when they misunderstand us as happened here, but we may not always notice it when we are in the midst of it'), one opens the door to more information about behaviour patterns as well as to alternative approaches to them. By acknowledging limitations the consultant makes it easier for others to do so. All the time, he acknowledges and works with the teachers' daily experience, from which he is, as pastoral colleague or outside professional, sufficiently distant, however, to act as a more objective outsider whose questions can throw light on or reveal gaps in their awareness and their unexplored assumptions about teaching and learning. If the consultant shares his knowledge in this way, teachers are more likely to examine its validity and to test out its implications.

At the same time, offering information as part of a process of joint exploration and genuine questioning is a teaching technique in its own right and likely to be of special interest to teachers, which they may be willing to develop further in their own classrooms, alongside other techniques which they employ.

Restoring objectivity

When personal feelings have intruded into the work situation, a teacher may find it difficult to deal with a pupil objectively. As we saw in the case discussions, a teacher may show that he prefers or rejects a pupil on grounds of positive or negative identification with him. This will cloud the teacher's judgement and influence the way in which he uses his authority. The teacher may over-react or even abdicate in the face of actual or perceived challenges to his competence if he himself harbours doubts about it. Alternatively, he may take a subjective stance arising from deeply held convictions about life and learning, and may feel under pressure from superiors, from pupils' parents or from what the public at large seems to demand of teachers.

The consultant will notice these problems only through what the teacher contributes to the discussion. He has to judge whether to use these contributions now, or later, when any tension has passed and alternatives have become clearer. The consultant thus tries to gauge the 'space between the words', between what has been said and what seems to be implied and between what may be purposely concealed, which has to be respected as private, and what remains unsaid because the teacher may be unaware of features which, if brought into the open, might turn out to be untapped resources waiting to be used.

Different levels of communication and their significance in the consultancy setting have been discussed by others. Schein (1969), for instance, differentiates between four areas of the self:

(a) the 'open self' (or what we are prepared to reveal about ourselves);
(b) the 'concealed self' representing what is deliberately kept from others (this, as Caplan also emphasises, has to be respected as personal in the consultancy process);
(c) a 'blind area' of the self (the 'blind self'; our blind spots) which we conceal even from ourselves but which may be noticeable to others (for instance, the consultant and group may notice when a teacher seems to add to his problems with pupils without realising it);
(d) an 'unknown self', unknown to the person and to others (Schein considers this part of the self irrelevant for the purposes of consultation — surprisingly so, since this unknown self can be the area of hidden strengths, skills, potentialities and is capable of being tapped in the catalytic process of consultancy).

Contributions reflective of all four 'selves' are likely to be made in case discussions.

There appears to be no difficulty about the 'open self'. However, communication which is too intimate and personal may present problems to a consultancy group. A teacher may, for instance, describe a child's experience openly as 'identical' with his own childhood experience, as happened in the case of a pupil whose learning was presented as impeded by an overdemanding parent who set impossible standards. The consultant has to resist the temptation to explore this further and to continue to focus on the child in question and the search for a solution to his problem, without appearing to rebuff the teacher's personal remark. Such identification with the child (noticeable through comments such as 'I know what this child is going through; it happened to me') may also distort the teacher's perception since, if the child's situation becomes linked with his personal vulnerabilities, the teacher may project his own feelings and problems into the child, and his activity on the child's behalf may be distorted. In the 'severe father' case, for instance, we learned from the teacher that he was unable to avoid speaking to the father in a rejecting, demanding tone of voice, which effectively prevented the father from accepting his suggestions. The teacher was helped to realise that, instead of fighting the father, he might be of more use to the boy by helping him to cope better with the father's demands, as possible signs of concern for his son's future. Changing his feelings about the father, the teacher then managed to help him to appreciate the very real efforts that his son was making, to discuss matters calmly with him, to acknowledge his concern and to help him to support the boy's gradual progress. Another teacher mentioned how irritating she found one of her girls, second in a family of three daughters ('like myself'), whose mother constantly compared her unfavourably with the two others when she spoke to the teacher, and the teacher herself responding to the girl as she said her own mother had done to her. The group explored how one might help the child to be less irritating and then to let the mother see the teacher's growing acceptance. This in turn seemed to make the teacher more relaxed about the girl to whose provocative negativism she could now respond calmly and construc- tively, managing what Irvine (1979) refers to as responding 'to the reality of the other person, with ability to perceive his qualities, and to feel and react appropriately', instead of colluding with the child's own tendency to distort her relationship with the teacher in accordance with her experience of a fault-finding mother. Conversely, in another group a teacher presented the difficulties which she had with an adolescent girl who, while getting on well with other teachers, singled her out as a convenient target for defying authority — while the teacher herself had been in constant battle with the new headteacher whose authority she resented. The group discussed, in general, feelings of defiance towards an authority figure and their impact, and whether one might find ways of eliciting and strengthening latent, more constructive, alternative feelings in such pupils, acknowledging but, in the process, also setting limits to the anger displayed. The teacher participated eventually in exploring how this might be done and thoughtfully commented on 'what an experience it is to be at the receiving end of such outbursts'.

Finding such workable solutions in itself tends to reduce the anxiety felt about a case, whether or not it is connected with the teacher's personal life. However, where personal remarks suggest such a link, it is possible briefly to acknowledge them with the respect which is owed to reflected past pain and to accept them as illuminating the situation under discussion, without entering further into them. The focus can then remain on the pupil and the manifest problem, preserving the consultant–teacher relationship as one of objective joint exploration. Throughout, however, the consultant has been communicating at various levels; he has heard the teacher's manifest message (as in these cases the boy's learning difficulty and the girl's irritating behaviour) and also noticed, without explicit acknowledgement, the latent message (about the children and the teachers' own 'harmful parent'), which was tacitly attended to (by seeing the parents' behaviour as a symptom perhaps open to modification if they heard of their children's progress in a way which also accepted the parents).

As to our 'concealed' and 'blind' selves, it is perhaps the most seminal aspect of this form of support that private or even unconscious experience which may be interfering with the professional task is respected as private, while its possible significance for the work setting is not ignored. Teachers often bring into a presentation several themes, such as their feelings about the child, the parents and the role of mothers or fathers, or feelings about themselves in relation to the school. They may do this wittingly or unwittingly. Consciously or unconsciously, a teacher may agree with a parent's criticisms of the school and yet resent his or her raising them but not feel free to discuss this in the group. There may be unresolved ambivalence if the teacher himself has attracted some of the parent's dissatisfaction, deservedly or undeservedly. In the exploration, one may be able to discuss in general terms the roots of dissatisfaction — one's own and that of others — and alternative ways of dealing with it, before looking at the particular parent's reasons as perhaps lying partly in the school and partly in him or herself. The school could then become a conveniently available target for the parent, the school having certain insufficiencies to which some parents may feel antipathy for personal reasons. It may be useful to consider alternative responses to other people's projections and perhaps to discuss parents' responses to our own insufficiencies and how we may attribute to them what we feel about our imperfections. Teachers tend to be staggered, relieved and stimulated by 'simple' suggestions that what others think about us may be seen as their problem, but our reaction to this is ours and may well affect their attitude. They are staggered because the relevance for most of those discussing a case is immediately appreciable; they are relieved because it is presented as universal, and stimulated to tackle what real grounds there may be in the complaints. This also helps to sensitise them to the anxieties underlying complaints which prove to be groundless, as was illustrated in Len's case (pp. 43–46).

All this appears to be well within the scope of a staff support group but, since objectivity, and not therapy, is the aim, any such discussion must remain relevant to the case under discussion and the professional relationship involved. This enables the personal side, concealed or blind at first, to begin to inform professional action in aid of the child's learning. We shall see later to what extent the parents can be involved in similar ways.

Seeing their own privacy thus respected, teachers find that they can acknowledge the privacy of their pupils and can develop an ability to respond to their special emotional needs without violating this. Scharff and Hill (1976) and Hill (1975) have documented one such approach with adolescents as part of the curriculum. Tony's case (pp. 14–18) showed how respect for this principle helped a much younger child to share his distress with his teacher without talking about it and so to cope with it better. However, secrets 'kept dark' and yet obviously accepted in the group in general terms — such as the fact that problems occur regardless of length of career experience — may become openly admitted, respected, survived and found worth sharing objectively. Teachers found that secrecy about unavoidable failures had in fact added to the strain, further sapping their confidence, when failure accepted and jointly examined helped to restore it. It had been used to illuminate the task and not turned into a judgement of the person.

Partial successes are frequently discovered within perceived failure, and resources from the 'unknown self' may become manifest and usable for deliberate strategies. An advantage of the continuous support group (of a length sufficient to permit follow-up discussions) is that teachers can become aware of changes in their perception and interpretations of a child's behaviour between the initial presentation of a case and follow-ups, and discussion can bring out new responses to a child's special needs. It then becomes clearer how the use or nonuse of our professional skills depends on what details we notice about a child, how we interpret them and how we may distort what we perceive and then narrow each new perception in accordance with past distortions. The hackneyed concept of the self-fulfilling prophecy comes to life through catching oneself in the act, when a child's behaviour is seen to change in response to changing perceptions and anticipations, as we saw in Dave's case (pp. 30–32). Teachers reported that their perception sometimes changed even on their way home from the meeting. On one occasion, a teacher found that her perception changed even as she was planning to present a difficult boy ('who had given nothing but trouble the whole year') to the meeting later that day and 'for the first time, strangely enough, he was all right to-day', his behaviour changing in response before he was ever discussed at all!

It is clearly crucial that teachers should be aware of the role that we play in the processes of selective attention which influence our judgements and should recognise how these judgements affect their objects, how our feelings about pupils, influenced by such selective attention, are communicated to them in our reactions and how our lost objectivity may unwittingly collude with the pupil's own predispositions and lead to a re-enactment of his situation. Britton (1981) has analysed how trying to resist such unconscious collusion may go against the grain of a professional worker's own emotional inclinations. Hargreaves' (1972) application of Laing's concept of 'meta-perspectives' to the classroom and the teacher–pupil relationship is relevant here, as it describes how both a pupil's and a teacher's perceptions, interpretations and reactions — all those 'projective efforts after meaning' — may lead them to ascribe the best or worst possible intentions to the other. Since Abercrombie's (1969) description of her teaching technique with medical students, there have been a number of attempts to achieve awareness of such issues through approaches to the curriculum. We shall return to this point when we look at the relevance of curriculum skills to meeting special needs. What matters here is that in the consultancy process a potentially vicious spiral of self-confirming negative projections can be interrupted and that teachers may find themselves able to start its virtuous counterpart. They are then in a better position to do what Wall (1973) has stressed as uniquely within their scope; with objectivity restored, instead of accentuating further the difficulties which may have created the special needs, teachers capable of getting through to the children can then offer them a consistent set of new learning experiences in a genuinely re-educative process.

Sharing skills

As we have seen, the skills which this requires are, first of all, the ability to see beyond the behaviour displayed, to *gauge a child's needs* which the behaviour may mask. This involves unobtrusive observation, appraisal (of how, for instance, assertive behaviour may mask a low self-concept (Burns, 1982)) and reappraisal as needs evolve. Secondly, *special bridging efforts* have to be made to reach the child's 'teachable self'. The teacher needs to be able to perceive and to build on what is good in a child, to listen and to share his experience without intruding, to express acceptance and to convey to the child unostentatiously that his words and acts are understood as signs of the child's anxiety. The child may be able to bear these anxieties because they are understood and they need then not interfere so much with his work and relations with classmates. His feelings are being made manageable through the opportunity of airing them with somebody seen as supportive. We saw how Tony's teacher (pp. 14–18) skilfully intervened in the child's crisis behaviour, offered him support while setting limits to the behaviour and helped him to start learning again. With these skills, she found the 'area which was free of conflict' and could meet 'the teachable part of the self' (Oakeshott, 1973a). This requires a third set of skills: the *setting of learning experiences and presentation of educational material* in such a way that these help to amend the limiting ideas that the child may have developed about himself in relation to others and to the tasks which he is set. This is done through encouragement strategies, the use of 'confirming skills' and of curriculum content and attention to classroom dynamics and to the special management of potential disturbance points in the educational system and educational institutions (such as first entrance, end-of-year changes, change of teachers, and changing and leaving school).

Teachers in the groups were almost invariably surprised at their under-use of quite basic techniques of encouragement and recognition which they said that they valued but which they 'forgot' to use with their most troublesome pupils — who, they admitted, needed them most. Gulliford (1971) touches on this paradox in his discussion of Redl's teaching techniques with 'children who hate' (Redl and Winemann, 1957).

As I have tried to show, if teachers are to discover and develop their ability to respond to special needs, there should be no prescription in staff support groups of what they ought to do. While the consultant helps them to focus on the underlying issues, he also helps them to see what skills they need to employ to ensure the learning experiences required by individual children. In one such case, for example, a teacher presented unresponsive, prickly ten-year-old Ivan whom he could not teach anything and who did not respond even to praise on the one occasion when he had unexpectedly produced some very imaginative writing about one of Kipling's *Just-so Stories* which the teacher had read to the class. Praising him for it the next day after he had had time to read the children's writings, the teacher found that Ivan was back in his shell. When this case was discussed in the group, the content of the story — 'How the hedgehog got his prickles' — was found to be revealing; only then did the teacher himself recognise the therapeutic meaning which the story had for the child, which he had failed to see at the time. The teacher could then find a way of taking the class into the theme of protection and survival, showing respect and admiration for the hedgehog's way of defending himself against danger, as Ivan had done in his writing. Rather than having his work merely praised out of context, it could be accepted as part of the work of the class. Some of Ivan's needs were being understood at a deeper level, and one could begin to meet them in new learning experiences with his classmates.

Again it was the teacher who was left to decide how this might be attempted. As had been the case with Tony's teacher (pp. 14–18), he used his skills as a result of understanding better a specific incident (note in this context Redl's (1966) account of such therapeutic communication particularly as emotional first aid (Upton, 1983)) and then as part of the general interaction with pupils in their normal school activities. The teacher did not need to get closer to the child than either of them could bear, a point which has been stressed as crucial for the therapeutic use of educational skills (Caspari, 1975).

Restoring confidence

Clearly, it helps to restore confidence if one can develop one's capabilities in this way. The teachers' confidence may have been sapped for various reasons. Some teachers could see how they had misinterpreted as personal challenges children's rejection of their teaching, and others how their own perfectionist views on what a teacher ought to achieve or is 'entitled' to expect from pupils had made them defensive and induced a sense of failure and incompetence when their expectations were disappointed. This had made it even more difficult to gain access to the children whom they found difficult.

The consultant ensures that the focus remains on the pupil and the manifest problem; yet, as was shown, he works at different levels of communication. While the consultant helps the group to deal with pupils' failures and successes, success and failure in general become a professional issue, indirectly helping members in the repair of their own loss of confidence and self-esteem. One finds that assisting teachers to help their pupils to cope with felt inadequacy and insufficiencies often means that teachers become more able to accept their own vulnerabilities and, by accepting them, to turn them into capabilities — without specific reference to any individual teacher. (We shall see later (p. 102) how a similar situation arose between teachers and parents.)

Most teachers seemed, until then, to have regarded success and failure, their own and that of others, in purely subjective terms, as a reflection on the person. Only now, some said, could they look more dispassionately at their difficulties, to see what these could tell them about the task in hand. It is clearly important for teachers to be able to do this and to understand the educational significance of helping their pupils to experience success and failure as showing whether or not one is 'on the right track' (Bruner, 1961), rather than seeing them as cause for reward and punishment emanating from an institutional hierarchy. Where the latter experience dominates, we may wish to demonstrate our successes and to hide our failures, with effects on our self-esteem, confidence and motivation — influencing whether we make decisions in obedience to authority or critically on moral grounds. The relevance for teachers of this issue was shown in Milgram's (1974) studies which suggested that what influenced whether people developed sufficient self-confidence to analyse the problems confronting them and to solve them appropriately or whether they merely wanted to perform competently on authority's terms had much to do with their past rewards for deference to authority figures. A school's authority pattern was seen by the researchers as one of the antecedent conditions which affect self-confidence and motivation to proceed with one's tasks in any other way than that of obedience (or irrational rebellion against authority) or to assist the development of a positive self-concept on the basis of which one becomes the arbiter of one's actions.

These are important considerations for any organisation which is concerned for the motivation of its members (cf. Argyris, 1963). They assume special significance for institutions whose aim is the education of self-regulating individuals capable of assessing their own positive potential. As is now increasingly recognised (Burns, 1982), unless teachers are themselves capable of such self-regulating assessment and in the process become more able to look for what is positive in their pupils, the way in which they are or are not acknowledged by colleagues and superiors continues to have an effect on how they acknowledge others and on what happens between them and their pupils. (The point that teachers should be capable of self-regulating assessment tends to be forgotten by those who suggest that teacher assessment could be tied to merit money links (rejected by Graham (1984)) and/or observation in the classroom by superiors. This not only alters the performance in the process but also polarises those deemed to possess the required skills and those deemed not to (cf. Montgomery, 1984).) Teachers found this an issue of absorbing interest as they examined specific pupils' interaction with them, assessing and improving their performance without being 'told' that they needed to do so.

Special needs: the ordinary curriculum as a source of new learning experiences

As we saw on p. 54, teachers found that what they learned in the group enabled them to respond more helpfully to all their pupils and not only to those selected for discussion. This is of significance with regard to the whole teaching programme. It has been put to teachers in ordinary schools that 'when we consider the need of maladjusted children to succeed in their relationships, in their basic learning, in the management and expression of their feelings, in learning more acceptable and satisfying behaviour, we can find guidelines for the adaptation of the school curriculum that will make it appropriate for them' (Laslett, 1982).

One of the problems in special education, and the prime mover in the debate on integration, has been the difficulty of providing segregated children with a full normal education as well as meeting their special needs. Meeting special needs in ordinary schools appears problematic only to those who see the children in question as 'different'. However, as teachers in the groups have found, children share substantial common ground whatever their needs, and what is offered specially to the neediest will be of relevance to others; the difficulties some children experience may point to more general problems in classroom interaction; and learning to respond more appropriately to their most 'difficult pupils' made them better teachers for all.

It is of great interest to teachers in ordinary schools to hear how writers on special education suggest to their colleagues in the special sector that their teaching could be much enriched if they adopted some of the developments in the ordinary schools' curriculum (Gulliford, 1975; Laslett, 1977; Wilson, 1981; Upward, 1984). They refer them for instance to the curriculum projects contained in working papers and teaching kits issued by bodies such as the Schools Council, which cover the range of subjects taught, enable teachers to take as starting-points the pupils' own concerns and emphasise learning by direct experience and relevance to pupils' interests. All these are 'features which special school teachers have long recognised as appropriate for children with special needs' (Wilson, 1981).

Similarly, teachers in ordinary schools are urged to examine the concept of the pastoral curriculum and its place in the education of all their pupils. This may be a distinct but overlapping part of that curriculum area which is concerned with the pupils' social and personal education (exemplified in *Active Tutorial Work* (Baldwin and Wells, 1979–81; Tall, 1985), *Developmental Group Work* (Button, 1981–2; Thacker, 1985), Health Education or Schools Council humanities types of programmes). Alternatively it may be regarded as 'an integral part of the liberal education we ought to be offering' to every pupil, 'an education which is both intellectually challenging and personally significant for the way (pupils) live their lives', in which pupils can examine solutions to *actual* difficulties in the shape of *typical* ones which are part of the human condition which they are learning to understand (Elliott, 1982). The argument (for detailed discussion, cf. Best *et al* (1980), Best and Ribbins (1983) McLaughlin (1982), Elliott (1982), Ribbins (1984, 1985), Wilson and Cowell (1984), Quicke (1985)) is that, if education is concerned with understanding the human condition, it has to allow and help pupils to apply such understanding to their own condition, as individuals expected to develop responsibility about themselves in their relations with others and that the pastoral curriculum has to play a critical part in providing for such development. This is in sharp contrast with the misapplication of pastoral care and provision for special needs as a form of social control, rejected as 'pastoralisation' by Williamson (1980) and Ribbins (1985), which perceives pupils' difficulties merely as disabilities of children who must be adjusted to an unexamined school environment. The argument for the educative potential of the pastoral curriculum is that there is a curricular discipline in learning to understand the human condition and the part which emotions play in people's lives and in learning to accept responsibility for one's relationships and behaviour in the face of obstacles and pressures.

As we have seen, however, teachers in ordinary schools, for various reasons, do not always make full use of their educational resources. They do not always place sufficient emphasis on these issues and those methods, activities and contents within the curriculum which would allow children with particular difficulties to experience themselves as more successful academically, socially and personally and which would enable them to learn to understand and manage their feelings and to build up a concept of self-worth.

We have also seen how, with better understanding of children's special needs, teachers could rediscover a child's 'teachable self'. Teachers became more alert to the opportunities in the general educational programme to design learning experiences which could help children to deal with the problems in their lives better (while respecting the problems as private), to feel better about themselves and to widen their understanding of themselves, their world and the possibilities and limitations of choice which are open to them.

An increasing number of practitioners — arguing like Galloway (1985), 'that specialists should act as facilitators in helping teachers to adapt the curriculum in the light of children's needs' — (cf. for instance Bulman (1984), Button (1983), Fuller (1980), Mayes (1985), Sewell (1982), Visser (1983)) are now discussing arrangements designed to strengthen this dimension of learning in the whole school, to extend some of the expertise of the special needs support staff (remedial, pastoral and counselling) to all their teachers, to enable them to help children 'without always giving individual help' (Marland, 1980) and to understand and handle their difficulties. It is being stressed that to initiate such arrangements through systematic supportive discussions with groups of colleagues may be considered a proper task for the school-based special needs support staff — more so than would be possible for any consultant from outside. Working with colleagues in this way and for this purpose naturally asks for particular skills and understanding (an issue to which we shall return). An awareness of the pastoral potential in the whole curriculum range, beyond one's own subject expertise, will be one aspect of this and, as Ribbins (1984) suggests in his review of Barnes (1982) *Practical Curriculum Study*, a crucial qualification for such support co-ordinators if they want to achieve credibility with their colleagues and to focus attention on what it may be possible to achieve 'pastorally' from within each discipline and related learning activities.

The teachers in our groups, for instance, found an increasing number of ways of introducing into the curriculum accounts of the kinds of experience which were of concern to the children. This enables children to speak of their own experience if they wish to but explores it in general terms as it is reflected in the literature or other accounts used. This has of course been advocated as good educational practice for many years. Time-honoured pedagogical procedure, however, still tends to keep school subjects separate from those 'basic themes which give form to life and learning' (Bruner, 1968), and this makes it harder to engage the children's personal knowledge, concerns and emotional energy constructively in their learning. The consultancy process helped teachers in the support groups to find ways of linking personal experience with curriculum content. In other words, of linking 'caring' with 'teaching' by presenting subjects in such a way that the children's life situations are unobtrusively included in the curriculum, at one remove and as part of the human condition which their education is to help them to understand. Teachers found, as research confirms (Staines, 1971), that this can be done in spite of the limitations imposed by an examination-focused teaching schedule and that such teaching need not — and must not — imply any lessening of conceptual rigour.

Arts subjects, English and other humanities allow children to get in touch with their own situations and their feelings about them, and teachers found no difficulty in examining such opportunities both in general and with regard to specific cases. In accordance with the special needs gauged, they explored how to create opportunities to help children to understand how people affect each other by their attitudes and behaviour and their own contribution to the quality of a relationship. They explored, from primary school level onwards, the potential of movement and drama (excellent examples are given in Meier (1979) in the case of movement; for the possibilities of improvised drama cf. for instance Chilver (1967, 1978), Davies (1983), Heathcote and Wagner (1979), Johnson and O'Neill (1984)) for helping them to understand and express feelings or anxieties liable to interfere with relationships and educational performance, to experiment with expressing the opposites of such feelings and to discover that people have at least some choice in how to react to situations. Role play and drama at all levels, alongside direct teaching methods, are found to be full of potential for methods of creating 'imaginary' worlds which illuminate the 'real' world which pupils are facing or are about to face when leaving school. There are seminal accounts and examples (cf. Scharff and Hill, 1976; English, 1984; Werner, 1984; Karpf,

1985) of the different ways in which teachers can help pupils to face the threatening as well as the hopeful aspects of the 'real' world in relationships, work and non-work, and leisure and parenthood.

Teachers agreed (as do Wilson and Evans (1980) that the sciences, too, can be taught in personally significant ways (cf. Ridgway, 1984) and that they need to be taught also as cultural, general education subjects in relation to human attitudes and values about people and things around them. They can be taught as knowledge gained by people who needed to solve and communicate about problems with which they were faced, just as the pupils are. This has been recommended in numerous Association for Science Education policy statements and by leading scientists (cf. Bondi, 1982) since the Dainton (1968) enquiry (adapting to present concerns what earlier advocates had expounded at least since T. H. Huxley). 'Science for life' courses, with their content of finding out about ourselves, can heighten children's curiosity, interest and respect for themselves as learners and can develop their potential for self-understanding, social involvement and responsibility. Working with computers can, according to some studies (Rowan, 1982), lead to an education in co-operation as children 'identify their peers as resources for help with computer programming'. In the support groups, teachers of geography, history and social studies considered how best to relate their subjects to the pupils' concerns and agreed that awareness of the impact of geographical, historical and social factors on human activities needs to 'begin at home'. They found it possible to show that the skills and attitudes of enquiry and interpretation of evidence which they tried to teach within their subject disciplines were equally appropriate to their pupils' daily lives. They found that at times they failed to emphasise this and began to incorporate in their strategies learning experiences explicitly designed to meet needs such as the development of self-respect, self-confidence and self-understanding. Since Bruner's seminal project on *Man: a course of study* (Bruner, 1968; Jones, 1968), a wealth of material has become available to teachers on how to integrate the educational and psychological–therapeutic elements in their classroom work and to help pupils to understand the impact of what they are learning on their daily affairs and their developing 'view of man's nature as a species and of forces that shaped and continue to shape his humanity' (Bruner, 1968).

Teachers whose main motive in controlling classroom relationships had perhaps been to facilitate the covering of a syllabus 'out there' and who had tended to perceive difficult pupils as grit in the machine began to include these relationships more systematically in the general curricular experience, without explicit reference to individual children.

This has always been good practice with infant school teachers who use make-believe play, discussion of story materials and dramatic work to allow children to 'experiment' with their own problems in the disguise of fictional or real characters and to use stories 'to introduce children to the world's literature, (but are aware that) each child will hear and take from it what relates to him and to his condition' (Brearley *et al*, 1969). Similar opportunities exist throughout school life, acknowledging pupils' involvement implicitly, including in discussion, at safe third-person distance, other people representative of the children's own relationships and the feelings which are part of them. (As well as designing aspects of the *general* curriculum so as to arise from the children's experience, teachers have also been able to help children to discover for themselves, at an unobtrusive *individual* level, what they may gain from books which deal with everyday and specific problems, adding such books to the school library. Wilson (1983a) includes in her discussion of 'stories for disturbed children' a list of those which she has found teachers use to good effect. In some areas, children's librarians have helped teachers to compile lists of books which sensitively show how children grapple with experiences of fear, pain, hope and disappointment as they face the problems of adults' tensions and quarrels, family losses and re-alignments. Cropper (1980) stresses the importance of using such books incidentally, and criticises those stories which come too close to the child's actual situation, portray too idealised a picture of relationships, moralise or contrive solutions which cannot speak to the children's condition or which in other ways betray that they do not accept their problems as serious. The books which do, and which show the problems as survivable, can also show teachers how their own sensitivities may be used in new ways when working with children under stress. An examination of the whole field of bibliotherapy in relation to children has been made by Crompton (1980).)

As teachers in the groups explored the situations of individual children, they also shared each other's experience of such approaches to learning, such as reading a story and asking an infant school class such specially designed questions as would help to make them thoughtful about themselves and each other ('what do you think the little boy was feeling?' 'what would you have felt, or done, if you had been there?' and 'what was it that made him first so unhappy, and so much happier later'). Similar questions can arise out of Schools and Health Education Councils' projects such as *All About Me*. Teachers confirmed the potential that they found in discussions which were sensitively adapted to the experience of children of any school age, on what makes people feel good or bad, sad, annoyed or hurt and whether we then sometimes feel like hurting somebody else or think that nobody can help us. Both self-awareness and sensitivity to the needs of others can be fostered in a range of programmes with starters such as 'things that make us laugh, worried or frightened', 'the best and worst things that can happen to people', 'what I would (or would not) like others to do to me', 'how I see myself and how this differs from how others see me' and 'what one can do to others to make them feel better about themselves'. Classroom relations and any pupil's self-esteem can get a boost in 'adjective exercises' where each child is asked to write or say something positive about everyone else or where ball or cushion games require the thrower to do so as he throws the object to the next child (cf. also Burns, 1982; Upton, 1983, for a range of programmes which aim at giving pupils experience of trust and of giving and receiving care and a self-concept developing from such new learning experiences).

One teacher found that her perception and relationship with an unmanageable 11-year-old girl changed when, after discussing her case in the teachers' group, she let the children talk and write about 'our fears'. She received a piece of writing from the girl which showed some of her anxieties and helped the teacher to see the child's behaviour in a different light. A secondary school teacher noticed the effect of such teaching on her class of 12-year-olds who in the past had mercilessly taunted the class victim as sissy but were beginning to respect him as actually courageous as he faced their daily taunts (cf. in this context also the 'tough guy's' two-line essay on the topic 'my mother's face' ('My mother's face is full of tears even when she's smiling' as quoted in Posell, 1984).

Another teacher spoke about a 7-year-old boy who answered the question, 'when we're unhappy, can we sometimes do something ourselves to make things better again?', by saying that he could 'give (his) sister a hug' — an insight of almost Spinozean proportions and an example of how children's awareness can be stimulated when we show interest in their problems. It also exemplifies the process of becoming educated in the sphere of the emotions (Peters, 1974) by acknowledging the feelings that children have, why they may have them and how one may deal with them (cf. Jeanie's case, pp. 33–35). Discussion of this in the group made the teachers consider the possibility of helping children to recognise their own and others' states of feeling and to understand that one can sometimes do something about these.

Recent research on children's developing conceptions and recognition of emotions (Harris *et al*, 1981; Walker, 1981) shows the extent of their readiness for such learning. It underpins what teachers can do by the sensitive use of story material (Fielker, 1980) and of any ordinary day's seemingly trivial happenings, rebuffs and hurts, to make children think about the different ways that people have of dealing with them and to help them gradually to cope with what comes their way (cf. Redmond (1975) for a fine example of using first-year 'Rosemary's crying; Valerie has hit her' in this way, and Salmon (1980) for a thoughtful discussion of such aspects of 'coming to know').

Such explorations can include all those methods that teachers have developed to educate children in what language can do, both cognitively and affectively. They require teachers to be willing to listen to children finding a voice of their own in the toings and froings 'from communication to curriculum' (Barnes, 1976; Barnes *et al*, 1969; Martin *et al*, 1976). The Warnock Committee considered language development to be even more crucial for children with exceptional needs than for children with fewer problems or subject to less stress. They need help to understand what they feel and to give words to it and to ways of coping. Teachers do not always realise that there is a therapeutic as well as an educational dimension to language development and that time is needed for learning experiences with language designed to encourage self-awareness and an understanding of responsibility in relationships.

Teachers drew each others' attention to the range of language material now available to foster these abilities at any stage of a child's schooling and in any subject (this can include subjects such as mathematics and modern languages (Wilson, 1981; Martin *et al*, 1976; Paneth, 1980) which are not regarded by all teachers as easily conducive to education for personal development). Methods close to an imaginative 'key words' approach base the development of language skills on words which come closest to the pupils' experience (Ashton–Warner (1963) refused decades ago to use 'primers (where) sorrow (was) such a disgrace (that it was excluded from) their artificial sunshine world'). 'Theme-centred interaction methods' (Cohn, 1969) can facilitate within subject-based curricula the discussion of issues that affect pupils' daily lives, while specially designed Active Tutorial Work programmes (Baldwin and Wells, 1979–81), *Role play in language learning* (Livingstone, 1984; Porter Ladousse, 1984), use of 'critical incidents' and Developmental Group Work approaches (Hamblin, 1975, 1978; Button, 1974, 1980; Thacker, 1985) have been developed to equip pupils with the skills and attitudes that they need to be able to cope with group pressures which can cripple development. Techniques have also been developed to help pupils to assume some responsibility for what happens to them in their relationships (Charlton, 1985), to reflect on the effect of their behaviour on others, to find more appropriate ways of expressing their feelings of anger and frustration and to become sensitive to and supportive of others in distress — thereby pupils educating themselves in mutual support skills (Lang, 1983).

Mentioning in their groups the range of language activities in which they engaged their pupils enabled teachers to add to their repertoire of possibilities of helping children to discover their ability to care, to handle frustrations and anxieties, to explore what they ought and ought not to do to others and to learn that to understand feelings of hurt may prevent retaliation and suggest alternatives. This could be done by suggesting to children 'talking and not listening' exercises in which they explored in pairs or small groups the effects of not being listened to. The children may practise co-operative language modes in non-defensive disagreements where they can discover that opinions can be rejected without rejecting those who hold them, that one can respect users of different language patterns and that one can arrive at compromise decisions and group consensus and still show regard for minority views. Discussions could be devised for the explicit purpose of developing negotiating skills in conflict management (De Cecco and Schaeffer, 1978) where pupils describe their own conflicts and themselves explore all the ways that they can think of to resolve them and, cognitively and affectively, learn something about impulse control, the consequences of actions and the alternatives open to them. Children can be helped to analyse the ways in which we use language, by adapting for instance for classroom use Bales' (1970) guidelines for verbal behaviour analysis. This was found useful for comparing intended and unintended consequences of the tone of voice and words used in seeking or giving information, supporting or disagreeing with another's idea or how we react when our own ideas are accepted, ignored or rebuffed, and the choice we have in such reactions. Children can then also become aware of how choices are widened when we understand the reasons for tendentious use of language in stereotyping, scapegoating, polarising and prejudiced thinking and the effects of mishearings, misinterpretations, or selective and distorting listening.

If teachers can consistently relate language activities to problems rooted in the children's own concerns, they will not only teach them something about the uses and functions of language but also assist them to develop sensitivity to the needs of others, self-respect and self-confidence as they learn to think about relationships, about what may disturb communication or limit understanding and about what they can do about this in their own situations. At the same time, in the acts of understanding, sharing and accepting, the children with difficulties in their relationships may feel themselves less misunderstood, less confused, less distrustful and more accepted.

Teachers alert to the educational potential of skills exercises such as these have also been able to note when their own use of language becomes educationally dysfunctional (cf. Barnes *et al*, (1969), Delamont (1976), Hargreaves (1967), Nash (1976); with regard to teachers' use of language with hearing-impaired children, see Wood and Wood (1984).) They are then more likely to allow themselves to learn *from* their pupils, in the way that a mother can learn from her infant 'how to speak to him so that he can learn' (Lewis, 1963). It is widely accepted that the effectiveness of workers in the caring professions depends on their responsiveness to the client's communication and their ability to adapt to the needs that he expresses. Teachers agreed that it is equally profitable for them to consider their ways of speaking to children in this context of susceptibility and accessibility, to recognise which language and negotiating patterns are enabling (cf. Flanders, 1970; Staines, 1971; De Cecco and Schaeffer, 1978) and which are liable unintentionally to close learning situations or to damage learning relationships, especially with their difficult pupils. Such understanding, the teachers found, has both educational and therapeutic value, but they also found that they themselves needed the support which they were receiving, to reactivate their abilities to apply this understanding in their day-to-day teaching.

There is then a considerable potential in the ordinary curriculum, not for offering children a substitute for missing experience, but for providing those 'educational opportunities of quality' which the Warnock Committee insisted (these have since been outlined in more detail by Wilson (1981, 1983b)) are of the greatest importance in the education of children whose special needs interfere with their progress. To be able to offer these opportunities, teachers need to be aware that it is possible to approach special needs through subjects and learning activities across even a 'national' curriculum, at every level of ability and age, and that such an approach actually enriches it. This would reduce the risk of falling into the 'whip-round model of curriculum planning' (teachers being 'asked to throw into the curriculum kitty what they can find to contribute'), rightly deplored by Marland (1984). A recent discussion document from the Secondary Heads Association (SHA) (Duffy, 1984) similarly outlines the possibilities of such enrichment for all children across the whole curriculum. Any child's special need can be seen as expressing more strongly the need of all and as forming a significant part of those 'basic themes which give form to life and learning' and which therefore ought to form a significant part of the curriculum content. However, as Brearley *et al* (1969) have stressed, this requires teachers who appreciate these themes and the part that they have played in their own development and who understand the framework of relationships which enables children to learn. Thus integrated, these themes become a potent help in the search for guidelines which teachers are urged to find for the selection and treatment of subject matter related to the education of all their pupils and a basis for the special set of learning experiences designed to meet the special needs of some.

In joint consultancy exploration we need only draw attention to the existence and importance of these themes in the general educational programme and what special needs they can help to meet. As we have seen, the consultant's task is not to offer an alternative curriculum but an approach to it through which these themes — suggested by teacher educators at least for a good part of this century — are activated in the teachers' minds. The approach, instead of suggesting therapeutic and educational objectives as incompatible, gives depth to learning experiences, whether they are designed for the whole class or considered essential in the specific case, and rather than 'separating the "problem child" from his "normal" fellows, whether by segregation or by labelling, reassert his fellowship with them' (Irvine, 1979).

Enlisting parents as partners

No matter how well a teacher may eventually succeed in getting through to a child, gauging and meeting his needs (and it has been pointed out how well a school may succeed in doing so even if it cannot involve the child's parents (Kolvin, *et al*, 1982) and how later relations can become therapeutic despite unfortunate earlier ones (Clarke and Clarke, 1984)), we have seen how much more a teacher may be able to achieve if he is in close touch with the home. The Warnock Committee re-emphasised the importance of establishing a genuine teacher–parent partnership. Teachers are also warned, however, by special educationists (Laslett, 1982) and family therapists (Box, 1981) that the parents of some children can have a vested interest in having a difficult child in the family and that many children find themselves enmeshed as troubled go-betweens between the two conflicting systems of family and school (Taylor 1982, 1984). Dowling and Osborne (1985) demonstrate the potential of a 'joint systems approach' which considers the influence that the two systems of family and school have upon each other in relation to a child's educational problem. It clearly affects the problem itself, and reactions to suggested resolutions, if the family sees the problem entirely as the school's responsibility, or the school sees it as the family's responsibility, or if both can be helped to work together on the basis of such mutual understanding and respect as can facilitate finding solutions to the difficulties which confront the child.

For decades at least, teachers have been alerted to the importance of close co-operation in that 'no man's land between home and school, a minefield strewn with explosive emotions and prejudices' (*TES* leader, 1 October 1982). They can find such co-operation difficult at the best of times, but especially when they should seek it because of a child's special needs. They may fear being overwhelmed by a family's problems and may fear to get involved, to seem intrusive or to offend parents if they refer to problems — fears which made teachers switch off in their talks with parents, even when the parents themselves hinted at problems that they wanted to share. In the consultancy sessions, teachers became aware of this and examined how they might use their professionalism more effectively in their relationships with parents, in a range of difficulties as wide and as complex as life itself.

In most cases, these relationships had been affected by how both sides saw each other and how they saw the child's needs. *Teachers* may see a poor parent–child relationship, parental problems, ignorance and apathy as causing the child's difficulties and blame lack of interest, lack of understanding or hostility to teachers as factors militating against co-operation. *Parents* may deny the existence of difficulties at home, accuse the school of being at the root of the problem and complain that the teachers give their child too little, too much or the wrong kind of attention. They may, however, themselves be anxious and seek an interview with the school but fail to get the advice that they hoped for or to act on that given. They may be at a loss for words with teachers who are unaware of how communication between them has broken down or could be improved, with 'the conversation becoming a string of accusations and defensive counter-accusations as either side tries to emerge as winner of the contest, with my son as prize' (Carly, 1984). Teachers will then fail to obtain the kind of information which might enable them to understand the child's and parents' situation better and may be unable to explain to those willing to co-operate how to do so or to motivate the reluctant to become constructively involved.

Sociologists and psychologists examining the socio-psychodynamic aspects of professional relationships have directed attention to the hazards in communication and co-operation created by suggestions of power, omniscience or partiality, whether assumed by one side or attributed to it by the other (Gliedman and Roth, 1981). They stress that the parents of children with special needs have a particular need for professional support but may also be specially vulnerable in the face of professionals who may appear to define their child exclusively in terms of his difficulty or may seem to attribute blame to the parents. They show how easily parents — with special needs of their own (cf. Jones (1985) for how acceptance of this can favourably affect a school's policy) which require but may not receive recognition — may feel demeaned, intimidated or threatened by well-meaning, but perhaps ambivalent, professionals. Others (Galloway and Goodwin, 1979) comment on the frequent breakdown of parent–teacher relationships over children's difficulties in ordinary schools and attribute this to the teachers' relative inexperience — in contrast with teachers in special schools — in working with such children's parents, who may seem inarticulate and inadequate, and may feel anxious or guilty for their suspected part in the child's difficulty. As Galloway (1985) also shows, teachers themselves can experience contacts with parents as a source of stress if they do not have the skills necessary to approach them with confidence. Increasingly, specific in-service training in how to improve understanding in this area is being advocated. As Mittler and Mittler (1982) point out, teachers, like social workers, need to be aware of the child in the context of his family as a whole, and to take into consideration the pressures at home which affect his progress. They thus need to possess and to *apply as teachers* some of the knowledge and skill of social workers in working with families.

Research into parent involvement consistently notes how insufficiently developed such skills are in teachers (Blatchford *et al*, 1982; Gipps, 1982; Cleave *et al*, 1982; Hughes *et al*, 1980). Teachers frequently appear unaware that they themselves can learn from parents (Tizard and Hughes, 1984), that work with parents is likely to be more effective if built on their 'equivalent expertise' and understanding (Pugh and De'Ath, 1984; Wolfendale, 1983) and that with recognition and encouragement of their potential and actual strengths parents are more likely to encourage those of their children (Irvine, 1979). Even at the stage of nursery education, where a large proportion of parents are in daily contact with staff, it has been found that the staff may mistake their cordial relationships with parents for genuine parent involvement. There was in fact little exchange of information, although both sides said that they would like to have more information from each other, and very little real co-operation. Misconceptions on both sides seemed to be preventing better communication; parents felt unable to ask the questions that they would have liked to ask, and teachers thought parents uninterested.

Others (Coffield, 1981; Quinton et al, 1982; Quinton and Rutter, 1984) have commented on the misconceptions entertained by some teachers and other professionals about parents' caring capacities, which can make teachers defeatist about being able to enlist them to help their children's learning. Coffield attributes such doubts to some teachers' belief in a downward spiral of deprivation. Knight (1982) records parents as saying that they 'felt thick' and 'put down', and Jones (1980) stresses how much parents can resent the teachers who appear to assume that parents are incapable of contributing positively to their children's progress. At the other end of this scale of perceived knowledgeability, parents known to teachers to be well informed about educational matters can also find relations with their children's teachers uncomfortable; professors of sociology have been heard to express fears of making teachers feel defensive and thus impairing their relationships with their child; mature student-teachers often think it wise, for the same reason, to conceal the fact of their training from their own children's schools — and then find themselves dismayed by the teachers' attempts to 'teach the parent'!

A picture, then, emerges of well-intentioned efforts and of obstacles to be overcome if a parent–teacher partnership is to achieve the conjoint support which children's special needs may require.

When teachers in back-up support groups examined their contacts with parents, they agreed that, on the one hand, they may well underrate them, disapprove, talk at them, fear to get too involved and then give too ready reassurance which may in fact close the communication rather than reassure and that, on the other hand, parents may feel overtaxed by demands that they cannot meet (Mittler warns teachers against suggesting to parents a parenting style too alien for them to follow). They also found that worries and uncertainties, due to socio-economic circumstances or to the parents' own childhood scars, may make a school's request to meet them feel like another threat. The teachers agreed that in all such cases there was something that they could do to ease the situation, at least about the style of meeting and the first small steps towards dialogue. Realising that their own preconceptions, judgements and reactions often proved a hindrance, they found it useful to examine these in relation to the case discussed.

Wherever it was relevant in a specific case discussion, teachers were able to consider what can take place 'between the words' when parents and teachers meet, what facts, feelings and fantasies may ease or disturb a meeting and what fears, anxieties or expectations may disturb and distort the intended communication. They could then explore what professional skills were needed to achieve the common objective of the meeting, which was that it should be of help to the child concerned. Clearly, such encounters should be reasonably pleasant for the parent. The teachers therefore needed to think about the feelings that parents may have about themselves as parents or about their children when they face a teacher and what feelings they may have about the authority assumed by others. They had to consider that parents may or may not wish to express the anxieties and resentments which can be aroused if they feel that their child is not liked, or unfairly treated, or if the teachers seem to assume that they know what is good for him. If parents doubt the teacher's quality or interest in the child, they may be worried about his future; unacknowledged doubts about their own adequacy as parents may be intensified by envy of a competent teacher or by fear of his or her rivalry.

Teachers confirmed that they have, as we have seen, various reactions to parental behaviour. They may be in considerable turmoil when they meet parents who appear to them to be failing their children and to find no joy in them and who reiterate hostile feelings about the child; this can make teachers fear further contacts, lest anything they say may be used against the child at home, as we saw in Teresa's case (pp. 19–22). They meet parents in conflict with each other in which the children get involved, others united against a child and yet others who 'want the best' for him but seem to set about it in ways which undermine his progress. They may hear parents praise one child to the skies and have no good word for his brother or sister. Teachers will naturally not know what deep-seated causes may have led to this rejection. Moreover, they may also not sufficiently understand the processes through which children contribute to the interaction between parents and children in such a way that some children come to be perceived as 'good', treated lovingly and behave affectionately in return and others elicit constant irritability and hostility from parents who cannot tolerate or adjust to their needs in a vicious spiral of bad feelings, where the parents need as much support as the children. Teachers will also know nothing of the damaged childhood which causes some parents to induce their children to re-enact their own early battles with teachers and the unjust world that they seem to represent; they cannot make allowances for what they do not know, but they can learn to suspect some such reason for parental hostility. Parents may even blame the child's bad behaviour for their own marital difficulties or seem to hold the teachers responsible. In Vic's case (pp. 27–29) the teachers could see this as an indication of the mother's need for support rather than for the blame or rejection she seemed to expect. Len's grandmother (pp. 43–46) directed great anger at his teachers who at first saw no chance of mollifying her, but her feelings towards them changed when they themselves ceased to reject her and saw her as a worried and suffering woman who herself needed acceptance and support. In another case it was possible to overcome a grandmother's hostile feelings to her 10-year-old granddaughter (whom she singled out as being like the hated daughter-in-law who had abandoned the family, leaving the grandmother to look after the children) when the teacher mentioned how much the girl needed a caring grandmother's help and how good it was for her to have this granny, thereby implying confidence in the grandmother inspite of her hostile feelings — an approach to the partnership relationship analysed by Irvine (1979) as both insight promoting and strengthening caring capacity.

If teachers want to meet parents as partners, they need to be aware of such pressures, but also to be careful not to interfere with a complex system of relationships outside their scope or mandate, as Rutter (1975) warns. They also need to avoid a defeatist view of their own and the parents' capabilities. As research suggests (Quinton *et al*, 1982) adverse conditions may or may not seriously affect parenting abilities, and the childhood deprivations of parents may be perpetuated or attenuated by later experiences of criticism or support. Whether teachers manage to initiate a supportive relationship or unwittingly collude with the parents' negative expectations, will at least in part depend on their own understanding of such issues and their reactions to parents' behaviour.

Teachers in the groups found it helpful to examine in general terms (i.e. without individual exposure) how easy it is to judge parents without full understanding, to see teacher–parent relationships in one-way terms of experts giving advice to laymen and to fear that lay people will find them wanting and reject or attack their authority.

Teachers could see how this defeated their aims by reinforcing or creating the gulf that they were trying to bridge. We considered the ambivalence which any one of us may feel about getting involved beyond our traditional professional boundaries and how we may take defensive stances against defensive parents, so failing to note their anxiety and to take account of their experience. Teachers could accept that, if we feel defensive about our own human insufficiencies, these feelings can make us a convenient target for a parent's anger or anxiety. However, if we accept such insufficiencies, we are more likely to be able to deal with them and to understand and accept those of the parents, no matter how repugnant they may sometimes seem at first. Instead of seeing a parent as totally uncaring, ungrateful or unreasonably demanding, teachers found that it helped to consider that the feelings aroused in them might be a reflection of the parents' own feelings and that the parents might themselves experience others as uncaring, ungrateful and over-demanding. This made it easier for the teachers to accept the parents, and to get in touch with their caring abilities, by manifesting a caring professional attitude towards them.

It seemed to be generally more helpful to work on some assumptions rather than on others: that parents have and can develop skills and that they care (this should be assumed even about blatantly rejecting parents, as Kahn and Wright (1980) stress in their discussion of the universality of rejection and the hidden acceptance in rejecting families); that parents want their children to get on and would like to get on with them; that, where they seem to hinder or not to understand, parents may respond to the teachers' awareness of their children's needs and their emphasis on the parents' importance to their children (a crucial point to make explicit as we saw in Michael's and Len's cases (pp. 25–27 and 43–46); that parents are better involved by hearing good news about their children than by the complaints which they may expect; that this is more likely to convince parents that the teacher is on their child's side and on theirs.

It was possible to help teachers to accept the parents' feelings — even, or especially, where these seemed to be directed against the child. Teachers found that, if parents with such negative feelings hear a headteacher or any teacher who has first accepted the parents speak well of the child whom they had so far singled out for the difficulties that he or she was 'causing' them, this sometimes helped them to take a better view of themselves and of the child (as had happened in the case of Dave (pp. 30–33) and of the grandmother just described).

Teachers thus appreciated that parents need opportunities to express their feelings and to find them understood and accepted by somebody who is helpful, non-judgemental, on their side and confident about their importance to their child. This helped the teachers to lower tensions, to reduce a parent's sense of injustice and to discuss with them how parents and children influence each other and how the pressures faced by parents — their lack of time, fears about employment or loss of job, and other family anxieties — can perhaps be coped with in such a way that their children are freer to concentrate on school work and not fall behind because of what worries the parents. Talk about their children's needs at school and how playing with them at home and talking and listening to them can help enabled the teachers to invite the parents' help as being important also to the teacher. Teachers were surprised to find how thrilled parents often were when their help was invited and at times sensed that, while they were discussing with a parent how they might together help a child (for instance in relating better to other children), they were also helping the parent with a similar difficulty (learning to relate better to other adults with whom contact had been a nightmare). (As we saw (p. 84), similar developments occurred between consultant and teachers and were recognised as a particular feature of the Caplan model of consultation.) They found that such support often gave new confidence, especially to single custodial mothers or fathers, who feared that they might not be able to cope on their own. There was no need to probe into privacy or underlying causes, or to exhort parents, and thereby to undermine their sense of authority. Information-seeking questions could at the same time contain oblique dashes of advice ('what are the things that you can be nice about with him at home?' or 'how does she react if you say something good about her while you are busy with the baby?') and sometimes elicited further light on what was wrong as well as pointing the way to its amelior-ation, without becoming didactic about the need to show love more openly or how to deal with discipline problems by setting limits as well as giving encouragement.

It was important, however, for teachers always to understand partnership as a reciprocal process and not to misunderstand it as a one-way process of offering parents information and requesting their help. Such information about the teacher's objectives regarding the child, how particular difficulties are being handled, how the child responds to this at school and how the parent might support the teacher's efforts at home (such as commenting encouragingly and trying to refrain from disparaging remarks) is clearly an important part of parent–teacher co-operation and can have impressive effects on children's self-concept and school achievement (Brookover *et al*, 1965–67; Burns, 1982; Nash, 1976). Partnership, however, also requires understanding of what teachers can learn from parents about children at home (cf. Tizard and Hughes, 1984), respect for the parents' experience and readiness to learn from the parents' knowledge of their children, how they see their child's needs and strengths, how they feel that these needs might best be met and what they feel they can contribute to this joint endeavour — especially so when parents feel overwhelmed by their difficulties.

Most of the family problems which the teachers mentioned had to do with the parents' own most deeply felt human experiences. Birth, illness and death in the family, upheavals in relationships through family break-up, unemployment or imprisonment of a parent, or a sibling sent away to residential school because of maladjustment or physical handicap are stressful events for child and parents and always entail a change in parental response to the child. In any of these, a teacher's unobtrusive informed support of parent and child can make the difference between coping and greater disturbance.

As we saw with Tony (pp. 14–18), children frequently 'know what they are not supposed to know and feel what they are not supposed to feel' (Bowlby, 1979) concerning a lost parent, whose loss they may not be allowed to mention to the parent who remains. This parent may disown the secret, prevaricate about the absence, 'forbid' the child to grieve, try to discredit the absent parent or prevent all talk about him or her. Such a loss, worsened by the parent's feelings, has been shown to be potentially harmful, as the child tries to shut away what is thus forbidden, which persists, however, and may impair his relationships and progress and lead to a sense of unreality, inhibition of curiosity and distrust of others. Evidence shows (Bowlby, 1979; Black, 1982, 1983; Goldacre, 1980, 1985) that support for child and parent can prevent some of these consequences if both are helped to share their distress and not distort communication between them.

Increasingly, teachers found that they could give at least some such support without crossing their professional boundaries or getting closer to the parents than either could bear without discomfort. In the case of two children in one teacher's class of 8-year-olds, the opportunity came when the mother of one of them told the teacher of her attempts to refuse access to the father — whose 'bad blood' she blamed for her daughter's unmanageable behaviour — and when the girl had started to taunt and deride a boy in her class for not having a father. This boy was denied all knowledge of his father, in spite of actual contact with the paternal family, whom he was not supposed to know. Both these attempts to obliterate the 'bad' parent were discussed in the group. The teacher and headteacher were able to help the mothers to accept that children want to know about their parents, want to be able to feel good about both of them and that this can improve their self-esteem and self-confidence and lessen the danger that a child will begin later to identify with the image of a 'bad' parent. In other cases, mothers agreed that they might need to reassure their child that the father had not left because of the child's naughtiness. Parent and teacher could then share incidents of difficult behaviour and how they might both treat it with patience instead of adding to it by fighting the child. Teachers were heartened to see how the school's support and a show of trust in the parent's ability to help the child to pull through often kindled in the parents a new enjoyment of their children.

Much of the research on the impact of divorce on children and families and the work of the conciliation agencies are concerned with the question of how to help both the custodial and the non-custodial parent to assist the children to 'survive' the break-up. While teachers have no mandate as conciliators, the support which they can give is clearly more than minimal. When new relationships had to be formed with formal or informal step-parents, teachers were able to help both parents and step-parents to become more constructively involved in a child's education. This Ferri (1984) suggests as being within a teacher's remit. They could assist distraught adults to accept that children may have conflicting feelings of jealousy or anger against the newcomer for having 'stolen' or usurped their parent's love and to think of ways of helping them to cope with this. As we saw with Vic (pp. 27–29), a step-parent may be unable to tolerate the child's difficult behaviour, especially if it becomes the cause of discord, and the child may test the ever-diminishing tolerance in his world, at home and at school, in search of some acceptance of his 'badness'. In Vic's case, the school was enabled to break the vicious circle and could give support to both Vic and his despondent mother.

In Jeanie's case (pp. 33–35) we saw how a teacher helped a foster-mother who feared that she was failing the child, by sharing their experience of her. In another family the absence of a disabled child at a residential school so dominated every aspect of life that only a talk with their other child's teacher helped them to realise the support he also needed. In a number of cases such as Dave's (pp. 30–33) the family differentiated between the favourite child and another, who was made to carry the family's frustrations. The selection of children for particular family roles (Box, 1981; Pinkus and Dare, 1978) is clearly, as Rutter (1975) has stressed, not something which teachers can discuss with parents. Awareness of such possibilities, however, has guided teachers' discussions with parents and helped them to make some parents more accepting. As recent studies suggest (Madge, 1983; Breakwell *et al*, 1984), even the effects of paternal unemployment — with the increased risks of material hardship, illness, depression and tensions in the family, fears of being despised and deprecated by the outside world — might be mitigated through an 'intellectual ambulance service provided by teachers, family doctors and psychologists' (Brock, 1984). For instance, fathers can be alerted to the good effects which the opportunity of better interaction with their children can have on their learning.

Joint exploration in the back-up groups thus confronts teachers with a wide range of home situations affecting a child's progress at school, and with as wide a range of obstacles in the path of parent–teacher partnership. They saw that many of these, often seen as beyond a teacher's scope, can still be influenced in support of the child if teachers know how to share their concern without intrusion, recognise parents as people with anxieties of their own but also with actual and potential strengths which need to be encouraged, and do not appear to define the child exclusively in terms of his or her special needs. As we have seen, teachers were often surprised by the relative ease with which some parents, whom they had thought to be entrenched and immovable, responded to their suggestion of an exchange of information and the teachers' belief in them and their children.

To achieve this quality in the partnership, teachers needed to become more aware of the obstacles which might interfere from either side and to apply their insights to overcoming them through quite specific skills, as it was possible to consider them in the support groups. Caspari (1974) summarised the skills required as:

- showing parents that teachers need their knowledge and help, to enable the teachers to be of maximum help to their child;
- sharing with the family that information which the parents seem able to accept, and encouraging them to comment from their own experience of the child;
- conveying that their concerns are recognised and shared.

If this is sensitively done, parents may see:

- how another adult relates to their child, which suggests how they could themselves relate to him, yet is sufficiently different, because of its professional context, not to be felt as a criticism of their own parental behaviour;

- that the teacher accepts their child as growing up and as capable of acquiring skills;
- that the teacher's care includes them, with their own needs and difficulties, as well as the child;
- that their active participation is enlisted in such a way that they experience some success and a new sense of effectiveness with their children.

It may seem as if teachers were expected to spend an excessive amount of time with parents, time which they cannot normally spare. However, the teachers in the groups did not necessarily spend more time than usual with parents but used their encounters more purposefully to establish an effective partnership. Such meetings were no longer left to chance, as had sometimes been the case, or to the initiative of anxious or irate parents, and the parents were approached with special care, so that they were less likely to feel summoned. Systematic exploration in the groups of what this implied led, as we saw, to better consultation with parents about their children's needs. Instead of ignoring the parents' experience, the teachers began to suggest how both sides might work together, each within their own possibilities, to help the child to progress. In the process, the parent, too, could receive unobtrusive support and could reciprocate the goodwill that was being demonstrated.

The teachers also found that joint explorations such as these seemed to enhance their negotiation and partnership skills in general, both with colleagues and with professionals external to the school. Follow-up meetings as long as two years later confirmed that these developments in parent contact and mutual support had endured. This confirms the findings of others who use the method of joint consultative exploration, that members of such groups, finding this approach satisfying, begin to adopt in their own professional relationships the skills demonstrated by those who act as supportive consultants to them (Caplan, 1970; Irvine, 1979).

We must now turn to these support skills in detail.

PART III
Providing Support: Guidelines and Tasks

6
Developing On-going Support and Training Groups in a Variety of School Settings: Role and Task of School-based or Outside Consultants and of Special Needs Co-ordinators

Knowing the obstacles

If we accept that in-service support and professional development programmes can help teachers to respond more appropriately to the exceptional needs of children and that all children ought to have teachers capable of doing so, we need to look at how part of the specialised knowledge of those qualified in the field of mental health can best be made available to teachers. In its study of teachers' in-service needs and programmes, the DES-funded SITE Project (1978–81) included an evaluation of the approach and some of the work described in these pages, as a provider's response to a growing need in which the teachers had requested support. They did not specify *how* the support might be provided and it was left to the provider to discuss with them, in the light of past experience and research evidence, what type of support was most likely to meet their own professional needs and those of the children that they were worried about. In their final evaluation the researchers (Baker and Sikora, 1982; Hider, 1981) referred to this part of the SITE Project as 'a very successful joint course . . . considered by teachers involved to have been their most worthwhile activity of the 2-year period of the Project'. They concluded that the success had to some extent been due to clarification at the outset of what it would and would not be possible to provide, what the teachers might reasonably expect to achieve and what ground-rules would have to be honoured in the process. Agreement was reached as to timing, frequency and minimum number of sessions needed to meet these expectations; this agreement, too, was guided by evidence available as to the pros and cons of possible options. Decisions about initial and developing group membership likewise involved the teachers from the beginning in discussing what structure and procedure might be of maximum benefit to the staff as a whole.

In the cases described in Part I, an outside consultant's expertise as a special needs tutor was pooled with that of the teachers. On p. 3 a range of services within schools and outside was listed whose staff are experienced in the field of children's special needs. All these are now being urged to share with their colleagues in mainstream schools their expertise and depth of understanding and to equip themselves with the skills required for taking on what will be for many of them a new role. This also applies to the specially qualified pastoral, counselling and other special needs support teachers who are arranging staff seminars in their schools, who may start pilot groups with like-minded colleagues willing to talk about current problems with children and who hope later to extend these to the rest of the staff. As we have seen, such teamwork with teachers requires from those in a position to develop it an ability to bridge the gap between classroom teachers and those with additional understanding of children's emotional, behavioural and learning difficulties and to demonstrate that their skills will in fact be of use in the classroom.

The ground for such support work thus needs to be most carefully prepared. For most schools a consultancy support group is a new experience. A potential consultant or staff workshop initiator — whether internal or external — has to keep this in mind to be able to appreciate what difficulties may impede such a new group's work. The findings of both group psychology and sociological analysis are useful to consider in this context of involving staff in their own in-service programme. A knowledge of the psychology and dynamics of groups will show how influences supporting the professional task may be strengthened, and those which interfere may be reduced (cf. for instance Bion (1961), Morris (1965; 1972), Rice (1971), Richardson (1967; 1973), Taylor (1965)). Sociological studies can help to illuminate the values and assumptions concerning interaction and purpose in education which underlie consultancy work. Of particular concern here are perceptions of the professional task and of the nature of problems and the question of whether and how these perceptions can or should be altered if found to rest on labels and typifications or ideological evaluations dysfunctional to the task. Much has for instance been written to alert teachers to the obstacles with which their own perceptions of pupil behaviour may confront their pupils with regard to self-concept, pupil career, access and opportunity in education and after school. Discussion is available of how such perceptions may be influenced by what sociologists call 'socially reproductive institutional perspectives', or the value judgements of society which are repeated and reinforced in the institution, but also how the resulting distortions may be redressed by attention to the teachers' awareness of their perceptions and attitudes in relation to the professional task (cf. Eggleston, 1977; Musgrave, 1979; Broadfoot, 1979).

Of special interest to a consultant offering to help teachers to meet the needs of children with whom they experience difficulties are those investigations concerned with the fate of innovation in schools and the frequency with which, because of social and institutional processes inimical to the change, innovations either fail to achieve their aims or come to an end when the innovator leaves (Musgrave, 1979; Shipman *et al*, 1974; Whiteside, 1978; Bell 1985). While, as Eggleston points out, this raises questions about the autonomy of the educational system and the individual autonomy of those who work in schools, the investigations also showed that the processes which prevented the innovation from taking root were not located solely in the institution; it matters that the innovator understands what the changes involve for all concerned and that he does not neglect to teach the skills and to foster the attitudes required to sustain the changes. A potential consultant needs to consider such matters from the outset, in relation to the whole of his undertaking. It is important for him to have an idea of what hurdles and snags he may encounter on the way and to be prepared to examine what went wrong if his efforts do not meet the success hoped for.

Abortive developments in my own experience for instance — such as groups which ceased prematurely or failed to take off at all — have retrospectively highlighted several crucial points: I learned that a selective offer to one school alone may suggest a lack of confidence in the staff, which acceptance — as they may fear — seems to confirm. I also found that, while the support of headteacher and senior staff is obviously essential, they may welcome the arrangement but may not appreciate the continuity of internal support required; they may set up competing events, either because they have forgotten when the group

111

meets or because they think it will not matter if some members have to miss a meeting for some other task. In contrast, I found that an enthusiastic headteacher may welcome the arrangement too readily, which can become counter-productive. In one case, a headteacher arranged for all the staff to attend, and it later emerged that at least some of them were coming unwillingly to comply with the head-teacher's obvious wish, and this brought entrenched staffroom tensions into the group. These and similar experiences elsewhere showed that it was essential for the headteacher to offer the arrangement to the staff rather than to appear to impose it or to welcome it too eagerly without sufficient discussion, that external agencies need to offer consultation to schools at least on an area basis, that their representative(s) and initiators from among the school staff need to have established credibility and that there should be no semblance of an obligation on any particular teacher, to avoid suggestions of his being seen as 'in need of help'.

There are no set rules for the composition of such groups. However a group comes into existence – through suggestion from a special needs post-holder, an educational psychologist, special education staff – or through being requested by the school itself as happens now under GRIST arrangements, the above experiences show that introductory meetings always have a 'private agenda' comprised of a variety of perceptions concerning any such development. Careful thought has thus to be given to the range of pressures and misperceptions, to prepare the ground favourable to a good working group.

Initiating a teacher support group

(i) First approaches within or to the institution

It is essential to give careful thought to issues such as these regardless of whether the would-be consultant is a specially qualified member of the school staff or comes from outside the institution. Either needs to be aware that he may for instance be misapprehended by some teachers as critical of their methods; this hazard must be tackled when the idea of teacher support is first raised. This may come in the form of a question or request from some section or individual in the school. Alternatively potential consultants may themselves be able to take the initiative by turning their routine contacts with teachers about specific children into some general comment on the difficulties which many children increasingly experience and the anxieties that they are bound to have which hinder their progress and are of concern to teachers.

They may then wonder whether teachers might like to share their experience and to explore with them, in a series of sessions, the range of such pupils in order to find workable solutions for them in classroom situations and may suggest that this might help staff and pupils, as has been shown elsewhere. They would at this stage have to outline what they had in mind, since staff may well expect straight lectures on 'discipline with disruptive pupils', 'the psychology of disturbed children' or 'how to handle children with special needs'. However well-informed and even inspiring such talks may be, most lecturers will have found that, although the audience may find them 'most interesting', some will feel that what has been suggested 'wouldn't work with Tom in my class'. This is exactly the difficulty which a consultative joint problem-solving approach takes account of, and this can be explained when one turns down a request for lectures or other didactic advice.

As outsiders, consultants will increase their credibility if they can give recognition to the difficulties with which teachers have to cope and can show appreciation of the skills with which they tackle them, to which the consultant may be able to make a contribution. In this way the consultant also forestalls being set up as sole expert or his knowledge being perceived as inapplicable to a classroom context. Where a specially qualified member of the staff suggests such joint exploration between professionals with differing expertise, the consultant has to remember that it is the expertise which is different from and additional to their own which teachers expect from him. Pastoral, counselling and special needs support teachers therefore face the particular task of showing that their special skills can support those of their colleagues, without distancing themselves so much from them as to appear unacceptably 'special'. Either way, they will have to deal with questions, many of them unvoiced, in the teachers' minds. (Laslett and Smith (1984) summarise findings with regard to such 'unvoiced questions' as 'will you listen; really listen?', 'does asking for assistance imply incompetence?', 'will you tell the boss?', 'does "help" mean extra work for me?' and 'can anything be done quickly, which will make a difference now?'). As members of a profession representing authority and 'expected by society (to be) wise, just, capable, competent, knowledgeable' (Taylor, 1985), teachers are uneasy about admitting to have difficulties to those who seem to manage or whom they may perceive as critical, as wanting to tell them how to do their job better or as likely to blame them for the children's behaviour. Both internal and external consultants will also have to explain that, while they may well be working directly with some of the pupils in collaboration with classroom teachers, it is not necessary to know the children discussed in their joint explorations or to know them as well as the classroom teacher in daily contact (in contrast with those pupils referred to them directly).

As has been shown, it helps an outside consultant if he can make his offer to the schools of a limited area, such as one or two adjacent neighbourhoods, so that no one set of teachers will feel that they are considered to need special support. Such an offer may be open to any member of staff interested; this is more easily manageable in primary schools but not, as we have seen, impossible at secondary school level. Those who already have pastoral, counselling or tutorial responsibilities may be offered workshops in which they would explore and be helped to develop the skills required to work with teams of colleagues. In either case it is important to recognise and acknowledge the expertise and interests of school counsellors, tutors and others with pastoral responsibilities, who are already likely to be committed to or interested in the idea of consultative support for the staff in general, as complementary to their direct work with pupils.

An offer made on an area basis is likely to lead to requests from some schools for more information. Although such requests usually represent a need, this may be felt only in some parts of the institution. It is therefore crucial to secure the assistance of the headteacher and senior staff by demonstrating (for instance through examples from support work elsewhere) that the aims of such innovative support are congruent with the interests of their school and would, by helping to maximise its professional resources, contribute to the furtherance of its professional goals. Their active support is vital to legitimise the potential group, to protect, as has been stressed, its arrangements against such hazards as simultaneous competing meetings and to allow the growing insights to be put into practice.

A headteacher may also wish to attend the meetings. This will be beneficial for short consultative 'taster' courses under GRIST* schemes. Where, however, such problem-solving groups are to become an integral part of a school's support network a Head's regular attendance could easily inhibit the process of skill enhancement by virtue of his/her position as assessor of staff competence. The consultant will then have to discuss this hazard to obtain the Head's agreement to become an ad hoc attender rather than a regular one. This must be done without appearing to diminish the headteacher's role in providing leadership with regard to the support work. It is crucial that both headteacher and consultant

* grant-related in-service training

accept the headteacher's lead as 'a major force in defining the work task (of support) and establishing the values that go with it' (Hodgkinson, 1985). Obtaining sanction for the group in this way forestalls a number of difficulties; if the headteacher is present at case discussions before an exploratory climate has been established, teachers may expect him or her to offer solutions before they have themselves examined all the issues underlying the problem — expectations with which the headteacher may unwittingly collude. Nor are all headteachers aware of the effects of their presence among their staff. As Hargreaves (1972) describes, it is very difficult for teachers to talk freely in staff meetings even with headteachers on the best of terms with them. He showed how teachers may try for instance to impersonate what appears to be the headteacher's ideal of a good teacher. However, one can find an equally strong tendency for teachers to refuse to 'put their best foot forward' in the presence of the headteacher and indeed to remain silent in these circumstances. Comments to all these effects were made when the question of inviting their headteachers to join was first raised in developing groups, and some teachers mentioned the risk that they might shape their case presentations and contributions with an eye to the headteacher. There are, then, strong indications that, in the first instance at least, the presence of headteachers or their representatives is likely to inhibit teachers in the task of exploring difficulties experienced with some of their pupils and particularly in discussing any emerging rivalries which are perhaps already dysfunctional for the school. (In my own experience, especially long-term groups do eventually invite their headteachers to attend at later stages, when they have established a way of working. Both teachers and headteachers then found the consultancy mode of working with each other informative and useful, adding a new dimension to co-operation between them.)

It is therefore advisable to remind headteachers who show an interest in the offer of a staff support group how crucial their support of the group will be but how their unavoidable role as assessors of their staff's competence is likely to colour the case presentations should they wish to attend. Most people find it hard to admit problems in their work to their superiors and teachers may thus find it difficult to speak of the matters with which the group should be concerned. Headteachers who had hoped to attend a group from the outset usually then accept that their presence might have an inhibiting effect. This accords with the findings about other consultancy groups (cf. reference on p. 67 to Daines et al, 1981).

It is also important to discuss with the headteacher the necessity of confidentiality concerning the details of the discussions (cf. the unvoiced question 'will you tell the boss?' listed by Laslett and Smith (p. 113)). This crucial issue can be presented in terms of the obligation imposed on members of any professional group not to discuss outside the group any information gathered there, unless this is clearly in aid of those concerned. This principle admits discretionary discussion between group members and the headteacher — whose sanctioning of the group is thereby also maintained and extended to its potential development into an on-going support system — and other professionals involved in the child's education and welfare but excludes any references to what individual members have said in the group (and thus takes account of the unvoiced question of whether the boss will be told). (This definition can also help the group later on in their dealings with other professionals, who have been found sometimes to withhold information from teachers out of a misunderstanding of the concept of confidentiality (Fitzherbert, 1977), when having the information might have helped the teacher to meet a child's needs.)

Details such as these constitute important items for the first stage of the negotiations, together with an explanation of the method of consultation and the function of membership (whether, for instance, it is to be open to any member of staff or is to be a group for staff at middle management level, with which some schools may wish to start the development of a staff support and training system). The second stage is then to mention the desirability of an introductory–explanatory meeting with the teaching staff. In some cases, headteachers themselves suggest this; in others, mindful of the likely misconceptions if such a meeting is omitted, the consultant will wish to ask for an opportunity to explain to the teachers what he is offering and to make sure that all understand what such a group would be able to offer and what, together, one may reasonably hope to achieve.

(ii) Introducing consultancy support work to the teaching staff

Once these matters have been clarified, work with the staff can begin with the headteacher's approval. Where a consultant is an outsider, some headteachers, after introducing him to the staff, may remain for the rest of the meeting. One can then, with their agreement, explain in their presence that they would not participate as regular attenders in the proposed group and that proceedings would be confidential. This helps to make it clear from the beginning to both headteacher and staff that one is not to be identified with the interests of either party.

It is useful if this introductory meeting includes, in a primary school, the whole staff if possible, and in a secondary school all the teachers who may be interested in attending a group and as many as want to hear about the work that it may be doing. This is in order to forestall divisions between those who may become members of the pilot group and those who will not. The aim is to set out precisely what it is one is able to offer and what the staff may reasonably hope to gain from it. It is important that as far as possible the whole staff are in touch with the arrangement and are clear about it, to ensure maximum communication, within the framework of confidentiality. If measures aimed at meeting all children's special needs are to be effective, all their teachers need to be involved.

It helps if one limits oneself to a professionally matter-of-fact terminology and avoids language specific to one's own profession. In addition, such semi-jocular terms as 'worryshop', used by some workers in the field, are best avoided. This has an unhelpful connotation of dilatory inadequacy and risks promoting fantasies about the group and its members. In order to be clear about the group's work, the whole staff requires concise, concrete descriptions of the group's purpose and procedure. They always find it useful to hear of disguised examples of cases discussed in similar groups and how they were dealt with; these should be chosen to illustrate common experiences with children regarded as difficult, the feelings commonly aroused and the alternative ways of dealing with these situations which were worked out.

Everyone must know what contacts there will be between the group members or the consultant and those outside and what their purpose will be. Everyone should feel that the group will not 'cause trouble' or 'want to change everything' but will support the school's educational task and will not antagonise those who do not intend to join. This enables teachers to accept that the headteacher will wish to remain in touch with the group's work and be informed by group members within the confines of confidentiality as outlined.

Divergent interpretations and possible misconceptions still have to be taken into account. If any partisan interests are suspected, defences will be strong. Some may fear to be seen as in need of help by their superiors, while others may have anxieties about an outsider or co-ordinating colleague, who might judge their performance or omnisciently read their minds — or, even worse, misread them. Yet others may hope for some omnipotence which will bring quick solutions to their difficulties. There will also be different opinions about the proper way to handle classroom difficulties, about whether any but the inexperienced or the inadequate are entitled to have problems and about further typifications of children and parents.

Whether or not such notions are aired, it seems wise to assume their presence. Without explicitly mentioning them, one can start dealing with those unvoiced questions (cf. p. 113) in the course of the discussion, as the main assumptions underlying the consultancy process are spelt out. These relate particularly to problem awareness and commitment to analysing problems and attempting to solve them, as criteria of professionalism. They can be outlined as follows:

(a) that, if problems are articulated while 'hot', in a structured supportive setting, they are likely to be clarified in the process, which may then suggest workable alternative ways of coping with them;
(b) that talking and listening to other professionals may raise our sights as to the possibilities of coping and increase our professional performance;
(c) that through such processes we can learn, without loss of face, when we ourselves unwittingly add to our difficulties;
(d) that such discussions can overcome the conspiracy of silence between colleagues, based on the assumption that teachers ought to have no difficulties and should keep them dark if they do, lest the admission should reflect on their competence — an assumption which is itself detrimental to the professional task;
(e) that, as in other professions, difficulties must be expected at any stage of a career and that the concept of professionalism includes constructive analysis of the reasons for any problem, so that it may be resolved;
(f) that this may also release our professional creativeness, tap unexpected resources within ourselves and enhance the support which professionals can give each other.

One can then briefly describe the structure of the sessions as, for instance, a sequence of:

1 case presentations, in each of which the teacher outlines the child's behaviour in school, the solutions attempted and their results as he perceives them;
2 gathering of additional information:
(a) through questions from the group about any further details which they might think relevant;
(b) by contributions from those group members who know the child

or his family and may know details unknown to the presenter since their contact has been in other classes, different departments of the school or other schools which the child or his siblings have attended. This additional information, being pooled, may well reveal additional factors contributing to the difficulty;

3 joint exploration of issues on the basis of all the information now available, including its implications for alternative approaches to the child, his parents, the whole class and the learning task. Such discussion is directed to finding educational means to modify and extend the child's experience.

This allows one to show how joint exploration and pooled experience enable the presenter of a case to take a fresh look at the situation and to decide for himself how to employ his skills in the light of increased understanding. It also demonstrates how each case explored in this way involves every member of the group, whether or not the child is known to others present, and shows how this can help them all to build up a framework for analysing and approaching other problems as they arise. With this objective established, there is little danger of teachers losing interest during the discussion of each others' cases (as happened in some of the groups observed by Daines and her team (cf. p. 67). Evaluation of results from the groups of two sample years referred to earlier (Hanko, 1982) has shown that the teachers did indeed find the exploration of their colleagues' cases — regardless of a pupil's age — as useful as that of their own.

At this stage of the negotiations, possibilities can be shown, misconceptions and false hopes can be dealt with and a base of receptivity be created both for the proposed group to proceed from and for the interest of its non-member colleagues. As one tries to convey one's understanding of the teachers' work setting and appreciation of their responsibilities, it is possible and crucial to show one's own expertise as supportive of theirs but also to seek to make alternatives thinkable.

Before the staff decide whether they wish to start a consultancy support group, one needs to make sure that the ground-rules and obligations arising from membership are established to forestall those difficulties already referred to. It is important here to give some guidance on optimum arrangements for the size of group, the range and function of membership, the length of the pilot course and of individuals' attendance during a course, the timing of sessions and the length of meetings. It helps if this guidance is seen to be based on experience with other groups of teachers — the consultant's own or that of others as more evidence becomes now available — in different settings (cf. p. 56 for examples of these).

As to *size*, on short 'taster' courses under GRIST or single in-service days one may have to work with the whole staff of a school, after an introductory talk. 'Fishbowl' arrangements (an inner circle working group, with an outer circle monitoring the process, changing over at half-time) can then accommodate larger numbers. For groups to develop as an integral part of the staff's whole-school approach, however, it seems that groups of up to 12 members (some of them core members, others with short-term commitments, as outlined below) offer maximum benefit of members' range of experience and expertise. Larger groups are known to hinder frank expression of ideas when perceived or projected feelings of the group may influence or prevent contributions. A larger group would also mean that the presenter of a case would be bombarded with more contributions from fellow members than he could examine; and the consultant might have to deflect an unmanageable number of anecdotes or assertive statements – to help the group stay with the case – and some members might become silent passengers. It would then be difficult for the consultant not to act like a chairman or seminar tutor on whom the group would be ambivalently dependent. This would interfere with the co-ordinate interdependence essential to the process of joint exploration.

As to *membership*, one can outline the advantage of heterogeneous groups, which may contain members from the network of schools serving one community or, if confined to one school, from the range of departments and career experience. In accordance with Eggleston's (1977) analysis of the influence of individual perception and interpretation on a school's 'ecosystem', consultancy group membership will be significant both as regards the *number* of people who will be reached as the group develops and grows into an on-going support system and as regards the range of positions and responsibilities which they hold. Schools will differ in their decisions whether this should best start with a group open to staff regardless of status and length of career experience or with a training group for staff with special responsibilities who then assist in the development of support groups across the school. All teachers are, of course, as 'grass-roots care-takers' (Caplan, 1961) key people, because of their psychological significance for children, parents and colleagues. Caplan also stressed the importance of affecting a significant proportion of the forces which influence individual and institutional emotional health and have implications for both administrative action and personal interaction. The effect of a support system on the institution as a whole will depend on the number and positions of those members of the hierarchy who have, by attending, developed their perception of their responsibilities with regard to children's special needs and the way in which they exercise them, both with individual children and with features of the institution which they discover to be detrimental to its primary task of education.

Depending on the length of course envisaged for the pilot group, the self-selection of members may be on both core and short-term bases, which increases the proportion of staff who can become actively involved. (For instance, a two-school group, limited to twelve attenders at any one time, with four core members attending for a year and with planned turn-over of eight short-term members at the end of each term, would be able to involve twenty-eight teachers from both schools. This would incorporate as many teachers as the staff of many junior schools, and more than the staff of many infant schools. A four-school group, with eight core members and planned turn-over of four short-term members at each half-term and end of term (illustrated on pp. 22–29), can accommodate the same number of teachers for twice as many schools. I have also found that a much smaller proportion of the teachers in a large school can form a significant bridge between members and non-members, provided that they have — or are helped to have, through the group's focus on interaction skills — active contact with their colleagues across the departments. At the comprehensive school referred to on p. 42, with a staff of over eighty, twelve teachers representing a good range of experience and subjects, at first volunteered to compose a group for one term, with the option of a second term and some staff change-over if desired. The option was taken up during the second half of the first term. Eight members of the group wished to stay with it for this second term, and four new members could be admitted. The sixteen people thus involved decided at the final evaluation meeting to organise a continuing staff support group, without external help, for the following year. This appears to have been successful, according to the comments of such independent witnesses as the staff of the child guidance clinic in touch with the school, and even led to the formation of an additional parallel group.) The scope for a single group is remarkably wide — especially if one considers the relatively small amount of time for which any one consultant may be made available in any particular school or area.

The advantages of heterogeneous groups, with regard both to range of experience and information about the pupil discussed and to range of members' expertise, may have become obvious when the structure of the sessions was discussed. However, these concern also the teachers as colleagues. Younger teachers have commented on the reassurance that they derived from hearing their seniors admitting difficulties regardless of length of experience, while older ones welcomed the infectious strengths of recent commitment to the educational enterprise and its challenges and also the reminder of the need of the inexperienced for their support. It helps to stress these features at this stage, both to deal with the unvoiced questions regarding the equation of having difficulties with assumed incompetence and in anticipation of the likelihood of needing to deal constructively with questions of status and length of experience once the group has started (cf. p. 126).

The length of the course envisaged for the pilot group will affect arrangements for membership. For some groups, teachers are able to decide on a two- or three-term contract with core members attending throughout and carefully planned short-term membership with turnover each half-term. Colleagues with additional knowledge of a pupil whose case is to be discussed, or colleagues dealing with sudden crisis cases, can be invited to attend *ad hoc*. To other groups, it may be possible to offer one-term contracts, with or without option for a further term. The most obvious advantage of long-term groups is that they are able to follow up cases and to examine how the children's needs evolve. They can thereby further reduce the ever-present hazard of 'confirming' children's difficulties through initial diagnoses based on a confusion of symptoms with explanations — or of defining the whole pupil in terms of the initial diagnosis of deviance.

Even short-term pilot groups, however, can show teachers that workable alternatives may be found for many situations which they had deemed beyond their scope (cf. the group described on p. 19). Interestingly, in my study of ten different school settings in the two sample years already referred to, teachers who attended a 1-year group for 5 weeks were more emphatic about their gains from attending than were those who attended seven sessions for one term in a group which ended with that term. This, of course, raises the issue of reinforcement from within the institution. The fact that short-term members of a long-term group could remain in contact throughout (they could for instance return for follow-ups and evaluation meetings and generally followed developments with great interest), also promoted more easily a climate of consultative support in the whole institution.

It is possible at this stage to mention to teachers interested in a pilot support arrangement of at least two terms, of core and short-term members, that these roles are to be seen as complementary (rather than just a matter of individual preference). For instance, new short-term members offer constant reminders of the range of problems and their reiteration in an ever-new guise, and core members give groups the necessary continuity. Core members also have the most continuous opportunity of developing those support skills which may enable them to consolidate a staff support system in their school. There was also evidence that they used these skills more effectively with other groups, such as feeder schools, pupils' families and other services in the welfare network. This kind of teacher support thus also offers pointers to ways of overcoming the traditional separation of services with their sometimes conflicting interventions (Welton, 1983).

A group structure which balances continuity with change of membership in this way is also able to cater for the frustrations of fluctuating membership reported by Daines *et al* (p. 67). It can do so quite purposefully as it also offers an opportunity to examine the implications for teachers of such changes in group membership, since similar changes constantly affect their classrooms and the school as a whole. A pupil who has been absent has to rejoin a group whose recent experiences he has not shared; new pupils, and teachers, join and others leave, and rarely is sufficient account taken of the feelings of apprehension and loss thus generated. Since most of us at least appear to take such changes in our stride, teachers can be unaware of how children's past experiences may make them vulnerable to such situations. Unaware of the sense of abandonment which children may feel, teachers about to leave often think it best not to tell the children until their day of departure and thus leave the children to cope on their own with the range of conflicting emotions which that entails. There are as yet few schools which require the idea of sufficient 'notice' to include the children, to work with them through these experiences of loss and transition and to give them hope for new learning because the good of the past experience will not be obliterated in their and the teacher's mind. References to this aspect of children's needs in the life of the school and their school life occur naturally where it is also part of the life of the group.

More schools are now trying to bridge the transition from one school to another, at least academically through meetings of staff teaching certain subjects. The consultation groups have found, however, that meaningful communication between schools about children's special needs (i.e. more than forwarding records about them) is equally important and valuable. A school needs to know which of its new pupils have been receiving special attention at the school that they are leaving and what approaches have been found to answer best with each child. Scharff and Hill (1976) make similar points about school leavers 'between two worlds' and make a case for anticipatory guidance during the last year at school and a curriculum which takes account of the heightened apprehensions, anxieties and needs at this time of transition. However, they also found that, because of the exceptional organisational pressures in secondary schools at the end of the academic year, teachers are often least available to their pupils just when they are needed most.

Teachers themselves, of course, may remember the 'deskilling shock experiences' with which newcomers to the teaching profession may be greeted by their more experienced colleagues and the lack of any usable support (cf. Cope, 1971; Collins, 1969; Hannam *et al*, 1976). As such experiences have ripple effects in the classroom, it is clearly valuable to examine the underlying issues. As has been shown (Foulkes and Anthony, 1965), the reception of newcomers can affect their self-concept and a critical reception maintains the closure of the group to outside influences. Support groups which combine long-term and short-term membership naturally bring such issues to attention, as change itself becomes part of the structure designed to meet its members' immediate and long-term professional needs.

As to *timing and length of meetings*, conflicts with the school timetable need of course to be forestalled if the group is not to feel constantly rushed. This can be done best if the consultant can offer a choice between 1 and 1¼ hours during lunchtime — provided that teachers are freed from competing commitments — and between 1¼ and 1½ hours at the end of the school day. With this choice, teachers tend to prefer the later time, when there are fewer distractions. More can also be achieved in the longer meeting, which teachers appreciate. Yet both alternatives have worked well in different schools. Whatever the arrangement, however, it is crucial to stress the importance of regular attendance for a stretch of time and of agreeing on starting and finishing times which every attender can manage. Latecomers would miss the case presentation with which the meeting begins and could therefore not contribute meaningfully or gain much from the discussion, while early leavers would forego the accumulative effect of the discipline and content of joint explorations.

Consultants to a pilot group are likely to find weekly meetings an ideal arrangement, allowing ten sessions per term to stretch from the second week of term to about the last but one. It seems a good idea to preserve maximum continuity while allowing for the additional

124

demands made on teachers at the beginning and end of term. Further-more, unfinished business which is bound to remain at the end of meetings has a way of 'working itself through' between weekly sessions, can throw new light on the previous week's deliberations and facilitates the development of a framework for the analysis of problems in general. With longer spaces in between, the sheer quantity of disparate happenings and demands which fill even a fortnight of school life can easily obliterate such connections or detract from their relevance.

If there is a virtue in accepting the unavoidability of loose ends at the end of meetings, it would clearly be unwise to leave too many to the space between meetings. This could be a risk in this kind of work if one were to follow the pattern of most external in-service courses, with their 2-hour meetings. Teachers readily accept a time limit of 1¼ or 1½ hours if one points out that one may 'get lost in cases' if too much time is given to their exploration. Also, an additional ½ hour at the end of a busy day may make all the difference between feeling recharged by sharing experiences and being overtaxed by the intensity of the activity. The time limit may also help members to accept that loose ends will have to be lived with.

When matters such as these are raised in the introductory meeting — by which time a sufficient number of teachers may well be wishing to attend such a group in their school — there are usually questions on what preparation a case presentation requires (cf. the unvoiced question of 'does it mean extra work for me?'). In our case there was no preparation necessary apart from verbal presentation of the cases' most salient features (cf. p. 118). Questions also arise on the number of cases that one might deal with in any one session. In consultancy sessions with doctors, Gosling (1965) indicates a preference for two cases rather than one per session, but consultants to teachers will differ on what structure they feel their meetings require. When discussing the case of a pupil, teachers need to consider a wide range of information, including the pupil's relationships with other teachers, with school mates and in the family. Gathering this information in the meeting and discussing its implications takes more time at first but speeds up as members observe the relevance and significance of information pooled and gear their questions accordingly. Thus a group at the beginning may need to devote a whole session to each case, but after a while may be able to consider two per session or to include one or two follow-ups. Limiting the initial presentation of detail to its most salient features also prevents overwhelming the group by more detail than they are at first able to handle but ensures sufficient time for thoughtful discussion. Emphasis on the relevance of every discussion to problems in general will reassure those who were envisaging a greater number of cases per session.

Having clarified these considerations during the introductory session — more briefly than had to be done in these pages — staff will then want some time to consider their implications for them, before work can begin with the prospective group members.

Work with the groups

(i) Early group meetings: fixed roles, hierarchies and expectations about the consultant's role

The consultancy model here adopted is based, as was outlined, on the principle of joint exploration within a setting of co-ordinate relationships. However, such relationships cannot be assumed to exist at the outset. Many teachers will find it difficult at first to adjust to this kind of participation, may try to assume fixed roles — from 'resident cynic' to 'rebel' and 'realist' — and there will be many attempts to perpetuate a hierarchy. Consultants will know that it is easier to handle such attempts sooner rather than later and may have begun to forestall them already in the introductory meeting (cf. p. 122).

Where the support group contains a wide range of career experience, there may easily be deliberate or unwitting attempts to reproduce the institution's hierarchy in the group. Holders of senior appointments may, for instance, rightly or wrongly feel that their younger colleagues expect from them ready answers or, as happened in one group, may try to influence the selection of pupils for discussion. Their authority may be deferred to or resisted by less senior colleagues. Either way this will hinder a genuine exploration of issues and of their implications for the individual teacher. A consultant will try to forestall such situations but may have to handle them as they arise (cf. Vic's case (pp. 27–29) on how the issue of hierarchy conflict could be used on behalf of both child and staff, without loss of face). Where the essential features of procedure were established in the introductory meeting, members can now just be reminded, without embarrassment to either side, that each teacher needs to select his or her own case, that there should be no interruption of the presentation and that eliciting further detail *follows* the presentation so that everybody is able to look at the whole situation and nobody suggests solutions before all available information has been examined. As the exploration proceeds, one can then turn contributions, made from seemingly superior or inferior stances or from fixed role positions, into additional knowledge which illuminates the case, irrespective of the status of the contributor, his length of experience, or the role that he has chosen to assume (cf. the discussion of Dave (pp. 30–33), showing how his teacher was helped unobtrusively to relinquish his fixed role). What Caplan calls 'the authority of ideas', rather than status, can then do its work, confirming for members of both high and low status the relevance and complementary nature of their experience. It helps if all of us, no matter how many pupils we have taught or treated, remember that we need to look afresh at each new case — similar to expert musicians whose playing will suffer to the extent to which it suggests merely a repeat performance.

With all expertise thus shared in the joint effort of fresh exploration, the problem can be returned to the presenting teacher, who is now left to approach it anew, assured by the support experienced and the confidence conveyed that a fresh start is possible. It should be no surprise that even probationers respond to being treated as autonomous authentic professionals and as part of a network of relationships across the whole hierarchy, which can support the competence of every member.

Dealing with expectations about a consultant's role

Expectations exist from the moment that an offer of support has been made and will be influenced by teachers' attitudes to 'support', by their work setting and, as we saw, by the way in which the offer reaches them. Groups may expect the consultant to assume a leadership role beyond the exigencies of the first meetings. The consultant is certainly responsible for ensuring the observance of the exploratory sequence. He has to ensure that issues are highlighted, that focus remains on the task and that participation does not become judgemental but remains supportive. All this demands a temporarily high profile which members may expect to continue. Group members' unrealistic expectations of instant solutions may further be reinforced in the honeymoon period by seemingly miraculous changes in pupil behaviour which are attributed to the consultant's knowledge.

Collusion with any such false ideas would clearly be detrimental to the objectives of this form of consultancy — the achievement of autonomy in understanding behaviour and working out the implications for action. Any such collusion would also interfere with the consultant's own sensitivity to how the case and the situation presented are being received by the group. For the group, this can only lead to disappointment. It is therefore crucial from the very first case exploration to stress that none of us knows the answers at this stage but that we together can collect further information which may help us to clarify the issues. If one can show appreciation of the teacher's difficulties as natural and understandable, convey confidence in the group members as professionals with their own expertise and show one's own courage not to know as a vantage point from which to proceed, it will be easier for the members to accept more realistically what expertise one has to contribute as being neither omniscient nor disappointingly useless, in exactly the way in which one accepts their contributions.

In this way, one can ensure that no member has to bear the brunt of criticism or becomes the target of unsubstantiated ideas for solutions implying judgement of his way of handling the case. One can take care that seemingly outrageous features of a situation do not swallow all attention, by inviting members to consider the less obvious aspects of the case, to find their interrelation and possible significance. One may have to check over-talkative members tactfully by inviting contributions, early and unobtrusively, from anyone who is tempted to carry the role of silent member. This attempt to forestall the kind of role fix which may hinder individuals from deriving maximum professional gain can also assist in helping teachers to appreciate the importance of avoiding role fixing in their classrooms (discussed on p. 73), when their efforts with individual children are so often blocked by classroom groups who fix them in a group role detrimental to their development.

Since the teachers are to find their own informed way towards workable solutions, the consultancy support group needs to contain from the start an unobtrusive element of training in that direction. This will include paying attention to the special skills of attentiveness — Reik's (1947) 'listening with the third ear' — which is crucial to the understanding of special needs as encountered in the classroom and between colleagues, in furtherance of the professional task. For this reason, too, it is advisable to discourage the reading-out of prepared accounts of cases, which would obscure the teacher's feelings about particular features and tends to make listening more difficult. Written notes just for reference, to aid presentation and exploration, can be very useful, however, and deserve support. In this context, one can also explain at the very beginning features of one's own way of working which may be misinterpreted, for instance where the consultant himself prefers to make brief notes during the presentation of its main points, for reference during the exploration and for later follow-ups. Such notes will also allow him, at later meetings, to help the groups to become aware of the extent of their achievements.

Groups sometimes expect the consultant, at the end of a first meeting, to summarise the main points of a case. To do so may not always be appropriate. It would for instance run counter to the aims of consultancy as outlined, if such summary were to offer only one person's opinion as to which points are essential, and would suggest a leader's assumption of consensus about a case which will need much further thought by everybody. However, it may be useful periodically to highlight, by summarising, the essentials of the *process* and *sequence* of exploring a case at the end of a discussion (such as how the group looked at a child's actual behaviour, tried to see it in the context of what was known about him and so on, as outlined on p. 46)), which can assist in developing the problem approach skills which teachers need to apply when faced with pupils' difficulties in the classroom.

On account of the need for further thought about the issues highlighted, there is also in these meetings no 'final' decision-making stage which teachers may at first expect. As the case remains the responsibility of the teacher who presented it, it is that teacher who now has to use what better understanding resulted from the session and to work out the implications for him or herself. This process is helped if one sees that each meeting finishes on a positive note. In the same way, one may have to reinforce the importance of this when teachers finish a lesson, dismiss children at the end of the day or conclude a meeting with parents (the parallels between consultancy and teaching skills have already been referred to *passim*). The case explorations illustrated in Part I show how these processes may develop at the different stages of a group's life.

(ii) Stages of development in the groups

The detailed accounts of the case discussions given earlier are naturally much abbreviated descriptions of what happened in any one session. With each case, teachers are encouraged both to follow a systematic course of joint exploration of the details reported and then to 'follow the material where it leads'. This way of working often calls for a considerable change of attitude and the development of skills which they may not so far have practised. Outsiders to the groups, such as headteachers, often noticed these changes, and participants themselves commented on them. They may for instance be reflected in a new degree of confidence and competence in presentation and discussion in general which members may demonstrate in the course of time. We have already seen that there can be a number of obstacles which may impede a group's progress. However, where these have been satisfactorily negotiated, a pattern of development emerges, which in template form, and at the risk of oversimplification which ignores individual differences, may be described as follows.

The consultant may find that, during early sessions, cases tend to be presented haltingly and cautiously and that the consultant himself has to elicit essential facts by a few questions and promptings. Children tend to be described in generalities, often without concrete detail ('a worrier', 'can't do anything on his own', 'always in trouble', 'a thorough nuisance' or 'an aggressive child'). Behaviour may be mentioned without reference to the child's probable feelings, while the teacher's own feelings may colour the presentation. The problem tends to be seen as 'out there', in the pupil, his home circumstances or the school system, or the teacher may blame himself in anticipation of expected judgements. The teacher may hope for or expect explicit advice on what to do but may also be ambivalent about the expected instructions and may accept with some relief the encouragement to use his or her own judgement on the basis of the issues highlighted. The consultant has to ensure that the group looks at these, stays with the case or comes back to it, examines the issues before formulating answers and considers assumptions about a child's behaviour without implying criticism of those who hold them. He must watch that the discussion encourages teachers to look at the implications and cease to see descriptions ('aggressive child') as explanations. Teachers may be staggered by the improvements in the pupils' behaviour which may follow their first attempts to try the ideas aired. The consultant must watch that he does not allow these changes to be attributed to his expertise since this would imply that improvements are the result of techniques which have been taught rather than of growth in understanding, must watch that such dramatic changes are not mistaken for permanent solutions to a difficulty, and that they are not expected in each case. In addition, it is important that their non-appearance is not seen as a reflection on the teacher's skill.

As the course develops, teachers will take note of the consultant's systematic interest in the antecedents of the incidents mentioned and in the child's reactions to those of the teacher and other children. They themselves include more and more objective details in their presentation of a case and refer more often to how the child may be experiencing the situation. This enables the consultant to assume a lower profile during the information-gathering stage, intervening mainly at the later stages to ensure the fullest possible examination of issues and implications. The teachers can admit uncertainties more readily, show enjoyment of their extending resourcefulness and describe how their attitudes to difficult pupils have changed and how their relationships with them improve. Such improvements are increasingly attributed to changes in their own awareness and to having shared a problem objectively. They can begin to 'ignore' the consultant in the face of their own acknowledged expertise. Encouraged to examine a child's whole situation and how teachers are involved in it, they more readily include themselves as part of it. They accept that even with back-up consultation problems will hardly ever go away overnight and that needs will evolve and require further observation and management. Also, they may generally admit that their own exploration of the issues involved is more valuable than merely receiving advice.

Skills may be used with increasing sensitivity, in relation to both child and parent. We saw how in Michael's case (pp. 25–27), the teachers talked about the respect owed to complex relationships and the importance of not pushing advice with parents, in line with their own experience of the consultant's similar approach to them. It is also of interest to note how newcomers to a group are able to benefit from joining it at this later stage and from its earlier explorations, their awareness and actions reflecting the stage reached by the group as a whole. Short-term members, too, are helped by the questions that others have learned to ask themselves and to negotiate the earlier stages of the core group more rapidly.

Eventually, presentations and explorations become shorter and more concise, as more shared understanding has emerged from past joint discussions. This makes it easier to consider two cases in one session. More teachers now give clear indications that they have already been using their extended skills with the new case which they are presenting, including this in the presentation. This, too, can apply even to new short-term members who joined the groups later but had followed their development through discussions with colleagues, before joining — a sign that members and non-attending colleagues were clearly helping each other. Group members referred to this spontaneously and consistently at follow-up meetings as long as one and two years after a pilot course.

(iii) Case follow-ups

When one mentions in the introductory meeting that case follow-ups will be an integral part of the work, teachers are usually particularly interested, as they can bring anything that they try out back into the group for evaluation, instead of being left to get on with it. This opportunity is clearly desirable and easier to offer where meetings follow a weekly pattern. The longer the interval between sessions, the more difficult this will be, as teachers will then tend to crowd each new meeting with ever-new cases.

A case follow-up provides the chance to take account of how children's needs evolve after their case has been presented and their situation explored and what further skills and awareness this requires from teachers. It means that teachers can be further assisted to develop the kind of climate in which they continue to learn from the child. Difficulties in ordinary schools are frequently aggravated by teachers unwittingly defining their pupils in terms of their own first spontaneous reaction to overt behaviour and by then behaving towards them in ways which reproduce the unacceptable behaviour that they are trying and have managed momentarily to correct (such as praising a child for improvement by contrasting it with his former behaviour, to which he then reverts — 'thank goodness, a good piece of writing at last! but why did it have to take so long?! — reminding the child, as Stott (1982) remarks, 'that he is forgetting his resolve to be bloody minded').

When cases are followed up over a period of time, skills and techniques can be developed to counter engrained habits such as these. Less faith is placed in dramatic improvements, and there is less disappointment when these improvements are not maintained and behaviour deteriorates. Temporary deteriorations can be appreciated for instance as the child's way of testing the teacher's changed attitude or as re-enacting behaviour patterns established from the past and too deeply ingrained to be overcome in a short time.

The intention to focus the teachers' attention on evolving needs has implications for the handling of follow-ups. Early in a group's life, some teachers may hesitate to offer a follow-up, especially if they have nothing spectacular to report when others are delightedly talking about miraculous improvements. Tempting as it may be for the consultant to share this delight or to praise the teacher for such improvement, one should make it clear that improvement will not always follow and that it is not the teacher's performance which will be evaluated but the child's needs and response to what has been attempted. In distinction to behavioural consultancy the Caplan model avoids praising group members' good results, as this would imply disappointment with a less good result as a reflection on the teacher.

To underline these points, and to lessen any sense of being checked for delivery of goods, it seems best to leave the timing of follow-ups to the teacher, emphasising the needs of the case. Instead of questioning teachers, as one might do as a supervisor, one can temporarily close a case, unanxiously suggesting that it be considered again when more is known. The group's genuine interest in how a case develops after their initial exploration, and the consultant's confidence in the teacher's ability to work out the implications and to re-examine the situation, are usually sufficient to bring a follow-up, without reducing the teacher's sense of autonomy.

It is also useful to remind teachers that 'cure' (with its unfortunate connotation of completion at a fixed point) is neither our aim nor within our scope but that 'care' and 'response ability' can release children's powers of self-repair and so promote growth and improvement (both 'cure' and 'care' having been conjoint qualities of the original concept of the Latin *cura*, now preserved only in modern language derivatives (e.g. curator, curé, Kur). Teachers thus come to share with the consultant both knowledge and skills related to each case from the first presentation to follow-up. As we saw, teachers were found to consider follow-up of their colleagues' cases, despite their not knowing the children, as useful as that of their own. If this is not the experience of all consultants (cf. Daines' observations (p. 67)) or one's own experience in every group, it suggests important implications for the structure of group sessions. It raises the issue of the use made of experience in the group, to aid evolving skills and self-awareness irrespective of which case is being followed through.

(iv) Interpretations and interim evaluations

'Interpreting' experiences in the group

As we saw in Part I, aspects of a case presented may be reflected in the group itself as it discusses the child's situation. In some instances, it may be appropriate not to attempt to interpret (cf. Bettelheim's (1983) criticism of many distortive mistranslations of Freudian terms, which includes the use of 'interpretation' for Freud's far more tentative 'Deutung') — but to comment on this, specifically or in general terms at group level, without infringement of the principle of consultancy as personally non-intrusive (since consultancy groups are not first and foremost self-awareness groups where members gather explicitly for that purpose).

Teachers who complain about their pupils' unpunctuality may, for instance, present the group with this problem by arriving late for meetings when they could have avoided this. One group had been preoccupied with the difficulty of getting homework from certain children. They themselves had been asked to answer a questionnaire for the purpose of evaluating their experience in the support group, but several members failed to return it. With some lightness of touch such parallels can be pointed out, and the teachers may be able to examine their reasons for their own failure to meet agreed requests; this may illuminate the failure of the children and the extent to which the teachers may be supporting the behaviour which they think they are discouraging.

A group which is usually lively may become withdrawn when a withdrawn child is under consideration and apparently unable to explore the problem. Similarly, groups may become hyperactive in discussing a 'hyperactive' child. The presenting teacher may be 'all over the place' in his description, and teacher and group may seem to set each other off with the same reciprocal effect as that between child and teacher. One teacher described how a pair of unruly twins drove her to distraction with their inability to stick to demands that she made. To the amazement of the group a colleague of hers, trying to elaborate her presentation of the twins, did so in such a way that it became difficult for the group to keep track of the case, having to deal with 'unruly twins' in the group itself. Such parallels are easy and useful to discuss and do not create counterproductive defensive resistance which statements can call forth from a seemingly omniscient interpreter.

Other parallels may be less obvious. In Dipak's case (pp. 39–42) the teachers had complained that their superiors would not listen to them and that this made them feel frustrated and hopeless. None of them noticed how similar this was to their response to Dipak. Once this was aired, they could appreciate the hopelessness which their response to the boy's irritating behaviour might itself have been generating. They could then explore patterns of authority and dependence between pupils and teachers and between teachers in the staff hierarchy. They could also consider why they found the boy's behaviour so irritating and how certain ways of demanding advice and help invited refusal from senior colleagues — and in this case the consultant. This made it possible to explore how such behaviour increased mutual frustration.

In Tony's case (pp. 14–18), the teacher became suddenly aware, as she was describing it, that she was responding to the child's crisis like the family, hectically keeping everybody busy in order to escape dealing with the problem. In contrast, the case of Dave and his teacher (pp. 30–33) illustrates the potential of delayed comment on the whole experience in retrospect.

The *timing of comments* is clearly important and requires careful judgement. It will depend both on the effect which the group's behaviour is having on the case exploration and on the effect which the comment is likely to have on the discussion; withdrawn behaviour (failure to discuss) or hyperactivity (disjointed jumping from one point to another) are clearly not conducive to greater understanding. In both cases the parallels with the child's problems were pointed out, and this facilitated purposeful discussion. However, with Dave's teacher it was better not to comment while he was feeling helpless but to do so later, when things had improved and the experience could be considered as a whole. To make these comments earlier would probably have added to his despondency and have increased his resistance to altering his perception of Dave. In Vic's case (pp. 27–29) we had both immediate and postponed comments. A fleeting reference to the way in which the headteacher and probationary teacher seemed at times to re-enact the kind of relationship which distressed the child at home and thus provoked a parellel response in the child was part of the discussion of a phenomenon known in other professions as well. This intrigued them and enabled them — without loss of face or need to climb down — to work more harmoniously together.

If such comments on analogies between the group's behaviour and that of the child under discussion are timed acceptably, they can, as we saw, further understanding of the child's problems. To consolidate such insights for professional use, however, may require greater detachment, such as can develop in spontaneous and planned interim evaluations.

Interim evaluations

Opportunities for evaluation and consolidation of insight may occur spontaneously during particularly 'good' or 'bad' meetings. They may also be planned for set times, such as mid-term and the end of term, as an integral part of the course of group meetings, to consider the effect of work in the group on the professional task. Again, as has been stressed, in contrast with some other forms of group work such as psychotherapy or counselling, there is in professional consultation no mandate for exploration of personal matters. Evaluation of any growth in self-awareness and its significance for the professional task must therefore not involve any intrusion into members' personal concerns.

Spontaneous evaluations pertain to phases and stages of development as a group may experience them. In our case these will to some extent be affected also by the stresses and strains of the school year, and there will be periods when it is appropriate to note how both previous experiences in the group and events in the school may be affecting the mood of the meeting. A group is likely to begin with high expectations and go through courtship and honeymoon phases, intensified by improvements in pupils' behaviour which may seem dramatic results of the work in the group. As such initial improvements are unlikely to be maintained, disappointment will follow as long as teachers expect a panacea for success and while they overrate success and undervalue the educative potential of disillusion and failure. The task of the consultant is then to make the group face this paradox, that periods of disappointment and depression can be valuable by making us think and promoting new capacity for concern and a renewed search for understanding (in the affective as well as the cognitive sense), both personally and professionally.

During such periods it is useful to point out to a group that one is not attempting to remove their depression or disappointment but to see whether one can find through it new capacities for understanding and toleration which may enable them to help children to cope with theirs. Such evaluative comments may themselves help a group to move forwards, quite suddenly at times. It was in one such 'depressed' session, for instance, that Michael's teacher (pp. 25–27) reported his improvement, following her earlier failure with him. This almost electrified the group into seeing both failure and success as part of a process, facilitated in the non-judgemental climate of consultation which neither overrates success nor undervalues failure. Teachers found that reflection on such phases in the group could also help them with their discouraged pupils.

At interim evaluations planned in advance for a set time, the groups will spontaneously bring up points as they occur to them. The points which come up this way, without prompting, will be the best indicators of how effective the support has been for its members. Such evaluations tend to have a developmental pattern of their own.

At the first of such evaluations, members tend to be concerned with what they feel to be of benefit to themselves as teachers. Having come to obtain practical advice for a specific case, they may say that they are now more likely to think things through instead, learning to be their own best advisers. Both the teachers' and the headteachers' groups attributed this to the effect of *sharing* their concerns in a situation structured to deal with them (in contrast, for instance, to staffroom moans about difficult pupils). This kind of sharing, they felt, helped them:

- to *distance* themselves from the difficulty as they tried to describe it to supportive colleagues;
- to *recognise* their own situation in that of others;
- to *refocus* their attention in the processes of questioning and examining, noticing how their own changing awareness then affected their relationship with the pupil in such a way that he could change his behaviour in turn.

Later evaluations tend to show a shift in emphasis, from being more aware of their *own* perceptions of others and the effect of their expectations on them to an awareness of what *others*, rightly or wrongly, might be expecting of the teachers and how such expectations affected both sides. During their discussions they had come to experience — rather than theorise about — the need to understand what either side may be attributing to the other, as a precondition for meaningful communication. During evaluation periods such insights seemed to be consolidated, cognitively as well as affectively.

The essential aim of such evaluation meetings is to help teachers not only to feel more hopeful about coping with difficulties but also to substantiate this feeling. Such confirmation is essential if 'understanding the other side' is to bear fruit with their pupils and with those whose support they need to enlist on the pupils' behalf, such as parents, colleagues or other professionals and officials in a position to affect a child's education and welfare.

(v) Endings and post-course follow-ups

There may be no 'endings' where a member of staff has succeeded in developing an on-going support system. Where the arrangement is a pilot course initiated and run by an outsider to the school, post-course follow-ups, in addition to evaluations and follow-up sessions during the course, will be important. This is confirmed by those who have examined the effectiveness of in-service courses (cf. Rudduck, 1981). Such follow-ups can help to preserve what has been learnt on the course as well as to facilitate further developments which may lead to an on-going resource and support system. This then raises a number of issues, first of all that of when and how to end a course and contact with a group, to aid such development.

An in-service support and training course concerned with the acquisition of skills and the development of understanding in the field of special emotional needs, as has been shown (Sutherland, 1964), is likely to assume particular personal significance for its members, enabling them to incorporate whatever they come to feel as of special significance to themselves, as insight into such needs and appropriate responses to them is built up. Throughout the course, there will have been ambivalent feelings about such learning, resolved to varying degrees in the process of exploration. Depending on how far they were resolved, participants in a course which links professional understanding and competence with self-awareness may for this very reason wish the contact to continue beyond the point of actual professional need (just as, conversely, others may leave the course prematurely before accepting the interconnection).

Towards the end of a course, earlier uncertainties may be re-activated, and members may again give the consultant all the credit for their improved competence and potential for change and hold him or her responsible for everything that they have learnt. Aspects of endings and transitions will have been examined in case discussions when pupils or teachers leave, and prospects such as return visits may be used to mitigate fears about separation. Now, endings and future contacts are aspects to deal with in the groups themselves. (A sensitive account of what beginnings and endings of a course of study may mean to pupils and teachers can be found in the book by Salzberger–Wittenberg *et al* (1983).

For reasons such as these, endings have to be prepared weeks ahead. This can be done by mentioning in good time the possibility of having follow-up sessions and trying to clarify their purpose, so that they do not become just a device for postponing the ending. Their aims might be to review the course and what longer-term effects it may turn out to have, to deepen understanding and to strengthen skills developed during it and since, or to assist in extending the climate of consultancy in the school through staff support groups of their own.

The first post-course follow-up meeting needs to be timed well, neither too soon nor too late; an interval of a term or so seems a good time. In one case, for various reasons, the first follow-up did not occur until a year after termination. The discussion demonstrated that members, while they seemed to have maintained the level of insight and practice achieved on the course (this was the group which contained Don's, Michael's and Vic's teachers), had felt abandoned. Better-timed follow-up with other groups led at first to intermittent contact with the consultant and then to a 'continuing conference', to which any member of staff could bring cases for joint exploration. After a year of such intermittent meetings (the consultant attending their regular meetings only once or twice a term), one may find that staff and headteacher have themselves become consultants to each other. This will be a good point at which to leave the staff to their own conference.

Some groups do not suggest that they would like to have a follow-up meeting (as was the case with the group who had discussed Teresa). Although it is preferable for contact to be continued by request, the consultant can also suggest a further meeting, as was done there for 6 months later, since their course had only lasted one term, had amounted to seven sessions because of several unavoidable interruptions and had ended rather uneasily. In this case, the interest thus manifested by suggesting a further meeting helped to relieve the group's mixed feelings. Wanting to find out after this interval what the teachers felt that they had been able to learn from an unduly curtailed course proved the consultant's genuine interest and emphasised that one saw them as partners in the evaluation, with full regard for their professional competence and doubts.

This is clearly an important principle for effective follow-up meetings, whether their function is to review the course and its results, to deepen understanding and reinforce the skills acquired or to extend acceptance of staff support as a human resource in the institution. All these uses confirm the teachers both as independent practitioners and as supportive members of an educational team — which may sometimes at least find it useful to invite somebody else as a reinforcer or a fresh stimulant. The outside consultant, however, will have to be careful not to become almost a member of the institution, so as not to lose the valuable outsider perspective. At its best, a school staff, with the help of their specialist colleagues, may soon take responsibility for their own in-service support training, and the staff may become capable of professional self-regulation and development, in tune with evolving demands and needs.

At this point we can summarise the role and tasks of a consultant to teachers and of the special needs or pastoral co-ordinator in the school wishing to develop teacher support facilities with his or her colleagues.

Role and tasks of consultants and special needs co-ordinators

(i) The special needs professional acting as school-based or outside consultant

Whether he is a specially qualified special needs post-holder or pastoral colleague on the school's staff or contributes skills and experience from another institution and profession, his involvement as consultant can be variably active according to requirements and developments in the staff support group and will be influenced by his understanding of the group's preoccupations or 'basic assumptions' (Bion, 1961). We have seen that in the initial stages the task is to establish a particular mode of working while acknowledging group members' expertise from the start and, in later periods of partial successes and disappointments, to continue to highlight latent strengths and to make the experience in the group usable professionally. Such periods call for greater participation, but in general the consultant meets the group members as partners and tries to participate equally with them. He must therefore forestall any semblance of wanting to tell others how to do their job and avoid the role of sole expert into which teachers may cast him in perpetuation of the perceived gap between them. His skill consists in not accepting this role — without thereby diminishing the value of the contribution that he is offering to make — and to forestall such ambivalent feelings as tend to arise when sole expertise is claimed by or attributed to one side in this field.

The consultant has to deal with these hazards from the beginning, by being prepared to learn from the teachers and to convey his understanding of the difficulties in their work setting and of how it can obstruct a teacher's ability to respond sensitively to children's emotional needs. This implies that one accepts the teachers' views of their difficulties as the essential and only possible starting point in a mutual pooling of expertise and that one does not ignore or override the knowledge which teachers have of child development and the learning process but perceives that knowledge as capable of supplementation by those with therapeutic experience. The consultant's special understanding can then be offered, not as superior, but as complementary and useful in the search for ways of helping children with special needs to achieve sufficient sense of personal worth to participate more fruitfully in the educational enterprise.

We have seen how teachers can be helped to achieve this through an extension of their own skills, educational means and inner resources and how the consultant does not think it appropriate to offer clinical diagnoses or to teach a modified form of clinical–therapeutic treatment. He tries to enable them to see for themselves what difficulties there may be in a child's situation and how they might improve it by using educational means to help the child to cope better and to activate the therapeutic potential in educational methods and relationships.

As we saw, the consultant's contributions are calculated to ensure that the explorations are focused on the child's actual behaviour and the responses it generated, on seeing it in the context of what was known about the child's circumstances and on gauging underlying needs and what provision of new learning experiences might help to meet them. These related to:

(a) the teacher's interaction with the particular child (such as acknowledging unintrusively what the child may be feeling or confronting him constructively with a difficulty, in a process of limit-setting and confidence-building);
(b) consideration of the whole classroom group (to ensure new learning experiences with others);
(c) the therapeutic potential in the day-to-day curriculum as a source for such new learning experiences;
(d) the skills of involving other adults (parents or other professionals) as partners, in support of the teacher's objectives on behalf of the child.

As with similar support and training groups (cf. Gosling's (1965) analysis), to be able to make his contributions effectively the consultant to teachers needs firstly to be able to hear, non-judgementally and non-defensively, what they feel about their task and about himself. Secondly he needs to create the exploratory climate in which these feelings can be used in support of the teachers' task. Thirdly he needs to make his knowledge available in a way which is compatible with the overall purpose of the group, to enable the teachers to find their own most appropriate solutions to the cases examined as well as to all those others not brought up for discussion.

The consultant as recipient

The consultant's way of listening, of asking questions, of using his knowledge and of speculating about issues and consequences is designed to heighten awareness about people engaged in the educational process as teachers or pupils, whose personal background is likely to affect their participation in that process. This awareness is

141

intended to facilitate the crossing of boundaries between them, without intrusion into a personal sphere which remains sacrosanct.

As active recipient of what is being communicated in the group, the consultant learns something about the members themselves, about their hopes, expectations and disappointments concerning their professional performance and especially about their painful emotions when they feel that they are failing with individual children.

At the same time, the consultant learns that he himself — like the group members in their role as teachers — experiences in sympathy powerful feelings of hope and disappointment. His method requires him to accept and work with these feelings in relation to the members' professional task rather than ignoring them or in other ways collusively re-enacting the teachers' own inappropriate behaviour. If the consultant succeeds in doing this, he may also be able to demonstrate authentic support — in response to professional rather than personal need — and so may help the teachers themselves to support children in special need, their parents or colleagues whose help they wish to enlist in aid of the child's educational progress.

The consultant is aware, however, that he is himself vulnerable to hazards which may make him less responsive and thus impair his ability to do this. Such hazards are, for instance, an excessive wish to be helpful, a fear of not being helpful enough and a wish to prove himself or to prove a point to a group. These may cause the consultant to make premature comments before he or the group can really understand the issue. He may give advice to teachers who perhaps already feel belittled by 'experts' and to whom he is supposed to show that, by having a fresh look at the situation, they may find some of the answers on their own.

Such advice may be seen as 'good' and, if applied effectively, may bring temporary seemingly spectacular results but may also lead to hazardous idealisation of the consultant. By 'helping' in this way the consultant will increase the teachers' doubts of their own sufficiency, whereas his aim is to reduce the grounds for these doubts and to build up their self-confidence. Moreover, admiration tinged with feelings of inferiority can, as we know, nourish envious ambivalence. Teachers may cherish for a time an idealised image of the consultant, which is likely to collapse at the first failure to achieve immediate results, giving place to disillusion and rejection of what he has to offer. Members may also lose faith in their own capacity to solve problems and fall back on the belief that there are no solutions — a belief which makes some teachers doubt and even appear to ridicule an offer of support to begin with.

The consultant will sometimes be tempted to side with either teacher or pupil against the other or to agree with both in seeing either the parents or the school as the cause of all the trouble. This, too, needs to be avoided, as it militates against non-judgemental exploration of the situation. It will be important for the consultant to make it clear that to acknowledge that negative feelings about children, or punitive actions, are understandable is not to approve of them and to insist that they must be examined as part of the situation. Failing this, his non-judgemental stance may be mistaken for approval. Another hazard is that, if he feels tired and drained in a session, he may fail to empathise sufficiently and may reel off his intellectual knowledge in unwitting collusion with those who use their intellectualism in defence against insight.

It is an essential part of this approach to recognise that such things happen in most teaching and learning relationships. The teachers will themselves, like the pupils, at one time or other have wished for more competence and yet resisted more knowledge for fear of its risks, will have dreaded incompetence and will have felt inadequate. However, they may have rejected this as part of both their own and their pupils' reality, instead of accepting such feelings as part, and part only, of all our selves and rediscovering those parts which want to learn and find new solutions. If the consultant can receive these feelings and give them recognition, with the authenticity of a professional prepared to use his own vulnerabilities and to be open about them in an unfussy task-related way, he may help the teachers in two ways. He may first help them to be able to own and accept their feelings and thus, secondly, to set energies free for competent performance as they discover that such recognition is a valuable means of getting through to children whose own anxieties have interfered with their progress at school. To the extent to which the teachers can themselves, like the consultant, become active recipients, they may become able to let children feel that they understand and accept their emotional uncertainties (as we saw with our teachers), make them bearable by such containment and help them to progress.

The consultant as creator of an exploratory climate
As we have seen, the consultative mode of working with support groups here described is introduced to the teachers as one of joint exploration within a relationship of co-ordinate interdependence. This way of working tends not to be a very prominent feature of hierarchical institutions, with their tendency to demand perfection from the leaders of institutions who in their turn tend to judge staff in

accordance with similar demands. The consultant is likely to be the target of similar expectations — influenced, perhaps, by the 'high-' or 'low-' scale post that he holds on the staff — but any collusion with them on his part would either prolong the group's dependence or lead to a rejection of his actual abilities as falling short of the ideal. He must therefore emphasise from the beginning the co-operative nature of the venture, designed so that the teachers as autonomous professionals find for themselves, but supportive of each other, workable alternatives to solving the difficulties with which children's special needs confront them. We saw how the consultant has to aim at the first meeting to achieve general participation in a process of joint search. He has to create a climate of confidence which suggests to teachers that they can handle their own cases and that the only criteria for evaluation are derived from the task. To achieve an exploratory climate, the consultant should be careful not to act like the kind of teacher who is eager to offer answers when expected to do so, needs to listen to the questions which a presentation raises in the minds of the group members, must receive these questions with respect and must see to it that the differing expertise of each member, together with his own, becomes supportively available for the exploration.

He has to be alert to the likelihood of hidden agendas which militate against an exploratory climate in the form of misconceptions and erroneous expectations. This includes any ideas about offering 'therapy' which some members of the group may hope for or suspect. He does not define group or individual therapy as his task but has a duty to help both the children and the teachers in their professional role. To the extent to which the consultant succeeds in this, he may well, as Caplan first showed, help the group members indirectly also personally, and to that extent he may play a therapeutic role without setting out to do so. The experience of a genuinely exploratory climate may well be part of the 'therapy'.

The consultant as teacher

Yet within this climate, the consultant has a teaching brief, which he may have to pursue quite directively.

Like other members of the group, he contributes his own complementary expertise; factual knowledge of child development and behaviour, and of disturbance-producing situations and the significance of various symptoms. He relates this to the educational context in which the teachers operate, extends their knowledge and skills and modifies their attitudes regarding the dynamics of families, classrooms and educational institutions as a whole and the interaction of teachers and learners. He adds his own professional way of looking at children to theirs, helping the teachers to define problems in interactional terms, and pools ideas of treatment alternatives which might help. The consultant can show how different approaches — within the teaching profession (teachers in secondary schools for instance are sometimes surprised by how relevant their infant and junior school colleagues' understanding is to the teaching of adolescents, and vice versa) and across professions — can be combined creatively in the teaching process when one thus focuses on underlying issues. He thereby helps them to stretch and define the limits of their role and responsibility more flexibly (a point which Maher (1985) for instance makes with regard to the school's response to juvenile crime), as he does with his own professional boundaries when redeploying his skills as consultant to groups of colleagues or interprofessionally.

As part of his boundary function the consultant helps the group to examine and develop the range of interactions within and across their professional boundaries — with members of the child's family and with professionals in the child care and other education services — and to discover how these may be better activated in the child's interest instead of interfering with it, as they sometimes do with unhappy consequences. As we saw in the case discussions, if the consultant's teaching brief includes focus on such hazards, and they are noted and understood in good time, they can be diminished or even forestalled. As has been shown, such teaching can take the form of both direct comments and indirect use of a group's here-and-now experiences, which may offer opportunities to develop better understanding and the skills needed to convert it into appropriate action. What the consultant does not do is to set out to change everything or tell them to do their job differently.

(ii) Role and tasks of the school-based special needs co-ordinator

Increasingly, among their own special needs staff, schools have in-service co-ordinators, designated colleagues with pastoral and counselling skills and some staff who hope to promote — as initiators, co-consultants and process helpers (cf. also the report of Baker and Sikora (1982) which arrived at conclusions related to some of those advanced here, being in part derived from results of the approach described in this book) — some internal structure and procedure which may facilitate the development of an effective special needs staff support and training system.

Such members of staff may themselves already be accepted by their

145

colleagues as possessing such skills as might be useful to share. They would thus be able to act as consultants to pilot and extended groups (a training element in such skills (such as task-related activities with colleagues in their schools) forms part of the special needs courses of in-service training departments) which they succeed in initiating as just described and be helped by such guidelines as already exist (e.g. the Schools Council's GRIDS programme (McMahon *et al*, 1984), or individual accounts such as those reported by Stagles (1985) and others listed on p. 12 which incorporate support work with colleagues). Alternatively, they may like to prepare the ground for such work in discussion with their colleagues and then, if enough of them agree, use their contacts with credible outside professionals to invite them to add their experience and expertise to that of the staff as temporary visiting consultants. As co-ordinators, they may convene a group of limited size but open to staff across the range of career experience, or one of key members of staff with whom it is hoped to build up the skills which they would need to run effective support groups with their colleagues. Consultants willing to do such work with teachers may be found in the network of external support services: child guidance units, school psychological services, special support and resource centres, special needs departments in higher education establishments. Special school staffs, too, can be invited to share with their mainstream colleagues their own expertise and depth of understanding.

Members of these services may lack experience in sharing their insights beyond their existing remit and, as Daines *et al* (1981) observed, may be diffident about assuming the role of consultant. They may be helped to assume this role by the co-ordinator on the staff who can discuss with them how best to ensure a successful start to a developing support system in his school. This will involve co-operation with the outside expert as a professional colleague to help him to find the most acceptable and workable approach to adapt his expertise to the setting in which the teachers work so that they can make use of his understanding within the constraints of a classroom, thus extending their own skills and resources. The co-ordinator will have to impress on the consultant the importance of clarifying with the potential group at the outset what he would feel able to contribute as an outsider, what, together, they might reasonably expect to achieve and what ground-rules would have to be agreed. The consultant will need to clarify with them the timing, frequency and minimum number of sessions needed to achieve these aims, who would be the core participants, what arrangements would be made for later or short-term attenders, what the pilot group itself might do to disseminate its experiences and what developments might be possible once the consultant's regular commitment expires. As we have seen throughout Part III, such considerations crucially precede actual work with the groups.

Through these advance discussions with his colleagues and with the prospective consultant, the co-ordinator demonstrates his partnership skills, increases his credibility with colleagues and prepares the ground for effective teamwork. This makes it more likely that a staff support system will become an integral crucial feature in the constant development of the staff's abilities to respond to their pupils' special needs.

If co-ordinators in neighbouring schools can agree to recruit consultants in this way the resources for supporting teachers will be greatly enriched. However, the potential consultants may themselves first wish to develop further their skills of support work with other professionals. Child Guidance Units have begun to develop a training role in consultation. Basic or advanced courses are run at places like the Tavistock Centre in London and in some university and college departments (also incorporating training in group work methodology in their training of educational psychologists (cf. Thacker, 1985)). Co-ordinators may also be able to induce the local branches of appropriate organisations or advisory services to set up workshops on support methods of promoting teachers' psychological insight into emotional factors in learning and failure to learn. (Organisations with an obvious interest in this field are for instance the Association for Child Psychology and Psychiatry (ACPP), the Association of Workers for Maladjusted Children (AWMC), the Group for the Advancement of Psychodynamics and Psychotherapy in Social Work (GAPPS), the National Association for Pastoral Care in Education (NAPCE), the National Association for Remedial Education (NARE), the National Association of Teachers and Teacher Therapists in Multi-disciplinary Settings (NATTA-TIMS) and the National Council for Special Education (NCSE).) Their London Branch is now offering courses in interprofessional consultation skills to Local Education Authorities, following the initiative taken by the Forum for the Advancement of Educational Therapy in running support and training courses for special needs post-holders.

7
Summary and Conclusions: Teacher Support and Pupil Care in the Context of School-based In-service Provision

We have considered the task of teachers in ordinary schools faced with the great number of children who need at some time during their school career more understanding than many teachers feel able to offer unaided.

We have reviewed the growing advocacy that professionals with special expertise in the field of children's special needs should include in their remit systematic work with more teachers than those whose pupils are individually referred to them. We have seen that such professionals, within and outside the schools, are growing more ready to turn their attention to support work with teachers. Since teachers are in the unique professional position of daily contact with these children, they have the opportunity to provide learning experiences which could enable them to cope better with their difficulties. It is increasingly agreed that teachers need such support in their work setting if they are to make maximum use of this opportunity and that all teachers should be enabled to do so. This book has been written in response to these demands, and in the light of growing interest in the possibilities, principles and practice of school-based in-service support and training.

We have seen that efforts to offer teachers the kind of support which may assist them to adapt their approach to children's special personal and educational needs are still isolated, and we have considered the obstacles which often interfere with the provision of such support. It has become clear that it is ineffective for experts from within or outside the school to deal solely with one child after another and simply to advise teachers what to do. This alone cannot take into account what goes on in their classrooms and why teachers often react to children's difficulties in unhelpful ways. The principles and skills with which the specialists treat such children have to be used differently if at least some of them are to become available to main-stream classroom teachers; the perceived conflict between therapeutic and educational objectives and approaches has to be reduced, and teachers need to be alerted to the therapeutic potential of educational activities. We have looked at how these specialists may deploy their skills flexibly and acceptably, with due regard to the nature of the obstacles militating against their efforts and to the factors which make for success in realising that potential.

An approach has been described by which suitably qualified professionals can, step by step, reach a maximum number of teachers through school-based group discussions in which they can gain additional knowledge and skills by focusing on the context in which they are to be used. In this way they can learn to cope with the behavioural, emotional and learning difficulties of more pupils than they can refer for individual treatment and to help the children themselves to cope better, thereby also obviating in many cases the dysfunctional stigmatisation of overtly special arrangements.

Teachers agreed that, when they had merely reacted to difficult situations without the necessary understanding or the skill to apply it on the spur of the moment, more often than not they had colluded with the child's difficulty and reinforced it, thus increasing their own and continuing rather than breaking the vicious chain reaction. A feature of the method was to discuss the difficulty in a way which took account of the teachers' need for both immediate and long-term help, by gaining new insights into difficulties, becoming aware of re-enactive patterns and learning to avoid further inappropriate reactions. This helped to free their energies and resources to design the new learning experiences the children could now be seen to need. In this process, teachers realised that the apparent gulf between therapeutic and educational objectives is not, as many had thought, unbridgeable, and this was seen to benefit not only the children discussed but also their other pupils.

Workers from the relevant disciplines, professions and institutions — potentially ranging from clinics to special schools, units, nurture groups and pastoral care systems — will have their own ways of marrying their expertise with that of teachers in ordinary classrooms.

While much still needs to be worked out in this field, the principles and skills involved in doing so effectively will not differ fundamentally, however, and need to be based — like those described here — on an appreciation of the setting in which teachers have to work. This means that such supporters should not see themselves in an exclusive expert role. They should be prepared to learn from the teachers whom they aim to support and whose knowledge and expertise they do not come to supplant but to supplement and enhance. They should understand the institutional realities of the schools whose staffs they are supporting if they want to help them to improve these realities, and they should accept the teachers' views of their difficulties as being of paramount importance and essential starting-points in the joint endeavour of pooling their expertise as autonomous professionals. They will thus not encourage watered-down applications of clinical expertise but will mobilise the teachers' own skills, educational means and inner resources by helping them to see for themselves what may be wrong in a child's situation. They will help teachers to recognise signs of stress and its different manifestations and to make better use of educational means to improve the child's situation by helping him to cope and by dealing with what is improvable in the environment (i.e. to recognise and put into effect the therapeutic elements in the educational system, educational methods, curricular content and educative relationships).

This method focuses on the teacher's and the school's educational concern with the child, alerting teachers to the influence of situational factors on children's response to the school's learning programme and to the opportunities which they have, as teachers, together with parents and colleagues, to maximise their own effectiveness in relation to the children who cause them concern (or would do so where unrecognised needs were understood better). The method is based on the inherent potential which can be activated in staff support groups which consist of a core of teachers willing to commit themselves to regular attendance of varying lengths (but also open to any colleague to attend on an *ad hoc* basis to discuss any child as the need arises). It thus not only avoids the 'special tension climate' of *ad hoc* meetings called together merely to deal with crises demanding immediate decisions but takes account of evolving needs and the pastoral care-taking dimensions of the teaching task.

As an in-service provision of support and guidance the method can thus help teachers to respond more appropriately to difficulties with children as they arise and to feel less frustrated or helpless about them.

150

It caters for the specific professional needs of the participant teachers. It can take account of each participant's need for information and release of the skills necessary to put insights and principles into practice. It does so at the point at which the difficulty is experienced and permits it to be examined in follow-up discussions of evolving needs, with fellow-teachers and a professional capable of redirecting perceptions. All are working together in such a way that the possible contributory factors can be looked at — including those of the school setting — and knowledge, attitudes and skills conducive to finding solutions can be extended for application both to the specific case and to similar problems as they arise. At the same time it enables key individuals on either side of the boundary between schools and the guidance and welfare network through better co-operation to over-come the incidence of separate and conflicting interventions (Welton, 1983).

As an in-service provision of training, the method accords with the requirements stipulated for appropriate professional development: to maintain the autonomy of professionals in a field where this is equally crucial to those who teach and those expected to learn from them; to include reflection on (Mitchell, 1985) and application of the new skills 'as close to the job as possible' (Bolam, 1982; Lang, 1983), 'on the spot and within the school context' (Briault, 1977), in the form of school-based 'management which is both person oriented and task oriented, which leads but also listens' and of 'participative decision-making and flexible policies' (Eraut, 1977). With the help of specially qualified fellow participants, teachers inform themselves and each other, update their expertise, sharpen their awareness of organisational and attitudinal obstacles and may enhance their performance without the easily counterproductive pressures of merit-linked assessment pro-cedures. They become aware of educationally wasteful habits and dysfunctional effects of conflicts between educational values and apparent demands of the system, as well as the defensive strategies they may themselves be using.

The school-based nature of the arrangements, if carefully prepared, gives them the essential institutional support. It minimises the difficulties experienced by those who take courses elsewhere, in communicating to their colleagues what they have learned and in trying to apply the new knowledge in the old situation. Instead, it brings the new knowledge into the old situation, where it is shared, discussed and examined by colleagues, with correspondingly greater impact. This can create a climate of commitment to on-going implementation; its school-based nature facilitates post-course support for the skills and attitudes developed, in the form of intermittent follow-through meetings. It uses the inter- and intra-professional staff community as an in-service resource, which facilitates purposeful co-operation and the mutual support needed for implementation, by allowing teachers to discover their importance to each other as colleagues and collaborators — a source almost entirely neglected in traditional away-courses for isolated individuals. It thus goes some way towards meeting the demands of those who acknowledge the need for continuous training and support (Anthony and Chiland, 1982) (Sayer, 1987) and towards demonstrating to a school its own potential for institutional self-renewal as an in-service training institution. Teachers learn more effective ways of asking for support, of supporting colleagues and of sustaining their ability for more appropriate response to new demands. (HMIs (DES, 1984), advisory and research bodies such as the Advisory Committee on the Supply and Education of Teachers (ACSET) and the Committee for Research into Teacher Education (CRITE) and headteachers' organisations (Secondary Headteachers' Association (SHA)) (Duffy, 1984) alike maintain this to be a vital function of effective in-service provision.)

As a method of task-focused analysis it permits dissemination of available research findings and theory, and critical application of advances made in the special education sector and internal and external support services. These are relevant to all teachers both on account of the wide range of children with special needs in their classrooms and the substantial common ground shared by all children whatever their difficulties. With this approach, such information can be geared to the teachers' current experience and professional needs.

An additional bonus must surely be the economical way in which this approach can maximise existing resources in schools and support services, by 'looking at what exists and strengthening and widening it to meet an extension of its customary tasks' (Wall, 1979). As regards the wide range of well-qualified support service staff within and outside the schools, it asks for a minimal extension of their role and that they should equip themselves with and exercise the support skills required for involving groups of teachers in examining the issues confronting them in their professional task with children whose special needs hinder their educational progress. The teachers would require firm support by their LEA to be allocated a minimum of staff time for group discussions to enable them to use this additional expertise to enhance their own. Investment in such a programme of teacher support and pupil care on a national scale appears to be both vital and affordable, so that teachers, as the only professionals in daily contact with all school-age children, can address themselves to the demands of the post-Warnock decades, the aim of enhancing the quality of all children's lives, in fellowship with each other, in the process of education.

Bibliography

Abercrombie, M.L.J. 1969: *The Anatomy of Judgment*. Hutchinson (5th edn.).

Advisory Committee on the Supply and Education of Teachers (ACSET) 1984: *Teacher Training and Special Educational Needs*.

Ainscow, M. and Tweddle, D. 1979: *Preventing Classroom Failure*. Wiley.

Anthony, E.J. and Chiland, C. 1982: *The Child in his Family*, Vol. 7, *Children in Turmoil: Tomorrow's Parents*. Wiley.

Argyris, C. 1963: *Integrating the Individual and the Organization*. Wiley.

Argyris, C. 1970: *Intervention Theory and Method*. Addison-Wesley.

Argyris, C. 1982: *Reasoning, Learning and Action*. Sage.

Ashton-Warner, S. 1963: *Teacher*. Secker and Warburg.

Baker, K. and Sikora, J. 1982: *The Schools and In-service Teacher Education (SITE) Evaluation Project*. University of Bristol School of Education.

Baldwin, J. and Wells, H. 1979–81: *The Active Tutorial Work Development Project*. Basil Blackwell.

Bales, R. 1970: *The Verbal Analysis of Behaviour*. Holt, Rinehart and Winston.

Balint, M. 1957: *The Doctor, his Patient and the Illness*. Pitman Medical.

Barnes, D. 1976: *From Communication to Curriculum*. Penguin.

Barnes, D. 1982: *Practical Curriculum Study*. Routledge and Kegan Paul.

Barnes, D. Britton, J. and Rosen, H. 1969: *Language, the Learner and the School*. Penguin.

Barrett, M. 1985: Consultation to subsystems. In Dowling, E. and

Osborne, E. (eds.), *The Family and the School, A Joint Systems Approach to Problems with Children*. Routledge and Kegan Paul.

Bell, L.A. 1979: A discussion of some of the implications of using consultants in schools. *British Educational Research Journal*, 5(1).

Bell, L.A. 1985: Review of Joyce, B.R. *et al. The Structure of School Improvement. Pastoral Care in Education*, 3(1).

Berger, M. 1979a: Behaviour therapy. *Forum for the Advancement of Educational Therapy, Supplement 12*.

Berger, M. 1979b: Behaviour modification in education and professional practice: the dangers of a mindless technology. *Bulletin of the British Psychological Society, 32*.

Best, R., Jarvis, C. and Ribbins, P. 1980: *Perspectives in Pastoral Care*. Heinemann.

Best, R. and Ribbins, P. 1983: Rethinking the pastoral–academic split. *Pastoral Care in Education*, 1(1).

Best R., Ribbins, P. and Jarvis, C., with Oddy, D. 1983: *Education and Care*. Heinemann.

Bettelheim, B. 1983: *Freud and Man's Soul*. Alfred A. Knopf, NY.

Bion, W.R. 1961: *Experiences in Groups*. Tavistock.

Bion, W.R. 1970: *Attention and Interpretation*. Tavistock.

Black, D. 1982: The role of the mental health professional in access and custody disputes. Presented at the Association For Child Psychology and Psychiatry Conference *Divorce and its Impact on Children and Families*. London.

Black, D. 1983: *Impact of Bereavement on Children*. ACPP Paper (presented at the Institute of Child Health, London, June 1983).

Blackburn, K. 1983: The pastoral head: a developing role. *Pastoral Care in Education*, 1(1).

Blatchford, P., Battle, S. and Mays, J. 1982: *The First Transition*. NFER-Nelson.

Bolam, R. (ed.) 1982: *School-focused In-Service Training*. Heinemann Educational Books.

Bondi, H. 1982: Why science must go under the microscope. *TES*, September 10.

Bowlby, J. 1979: On Knowing What You Are Not Supposed to Know and Feeling What You Are Not Supposed to Feel. *Forum for the Advancement of Educational Therapy, Supplement 14*.

Bowlby, J. 1985: Foreword. In Dowling, E. and Osborne, E. (eds.) *The Family and the School, A Joint Systems Approach to Problems with Children*. Routledge and Kegan Paul.

Box, S. (ed.) 1981: *Psychotherapy with Families*. Routledge and Kegan Paul.

Boyle, J. 1977: *A Sense of Freedom*. Canongate.

Breakwell, G.M., Collie, A., Harrison, B. and Propper, C. 1984: Attitudes towards the unemployed: effects of threatened identity. *British Journal of Social Psychology*, 23 (February).

Brearley, M., Bott, R., Davies, M., Hitchfield, E., Johnson, J., Jones, W. and Tamburrini, J. 1969: *Fundamentals in the First School*. Blackwell.

Briault, E.W.H. 1977: Developing in-service education. *British Journal of In-Service Education*, (May).

Britton, R. 1981: Re-enactment as an unwitting professional response to family dynamics. In Box, S. (ed.) *Psychotherapy with Families*, Routledge and Kegan Paul.

Broadfoot, P. 1979: *Assessment, Schools and Society*. Methuen.

Brock, P. 1984: Unemployment: much more than an economic and social ill. *The Guardian*, April 25.

Brookover, W.B., Erickson, E.L. and Joiner, L.M. 1965–7: *Self-concept of Ability and School Achievement*. Educational Publishing Services, College of Education, University of Michigan.

Bruner, J.S. 1961: The act of discovery. *Harvard Educational Review*, 31(1).

Bruner, J.S. 1968: *Toward a Theory of Instruction*. Norton.

Bulman, L. 1984: The relationship between the pastoral curriculum, the academic curriculum, and the pastoral programme. *Pastoral Care in Education*, 2(2).

Burns, R. 1982: *Self-concept Development and Education*. Holt, Rinehart and Winston.

Button, L. 1974: *Developmental Group Work with Adolescents*. ULP.

Button, L. 1980: The skills of group tutoring. In Best, R., Jarvis, C. and Ribbins, P. (eds.) 1980: *Perspectives in Pastoral Care*. Heinemann.

Button, L. 1981–2: *Group Tutoring for the Form Teacher*. Hodder and Stoughton, Books 1 and 2.

Button, L. 1983: The pastoral curriculum. *Pastoral Care in Education*, 1(2).

Caplan, G. 1961: *An Approach to Community Mental Health*. Tavistock.

Caplan, G. 1970: *The Theory and Practice of Mental Health Consultation*. Basic Books.

Caplan, R. 1982: *Introduction to Schulberg, H.C. and Killilea, M. (eds.), The Modern Practice of Community Mental Health*. Jossey-Bass.

Carly, E. 1984: Special pleading. *The Guardian*, January 31.

Caspari, I. 1962: Problems of school consultation. *The New Era,* April.

Caspari, I. 1974: Parents as co-therapists. *International Congress of Child Psychiatry, Philadelphia, 1974* and *Forum for the Advancement of Educational Therapy, Supplement 2.*

Caspari, I. 1975: A psychodynamic view of the therapeutic opportunities of special education. In Wedell, K. (ed.). *Orientations in Special Education.* Wiley.

Caspari, I. 1976: *Troublesome Children in Class*, Chapter 12, Supervisory groups for teachers. Routledge and Kegan Paul.

Chandler, E. 1980: *Educating Adolescent Girls.* Allen and Unwin.

Charlton, T. 1985: Locus of control as a therapeutic strategy for helping children with behaviour and learning problems. *Maladjustment and Therapeutic Education*, 3(1).

Chilver, P. 1967: *Improvised Drama.* Batsford.

Chilver, P. 1978: *Teaching Improvised Drama.* Batsford.

Clarke, A.D.B. and Clarke, A.M. 1984: Constancy and change in the growth of human characteristics. *Journal of Child Psychology and Psychiatry*, 25(2).

Cleave, S., Jowett, S. and Bate, M. 1982: *And so to School . . .* NFER-Nelson.

Cline, T. 1980: More help for schools — a critical look at child guidance. *Therapeutic Education*, 8(1).

Clunies-Ross, L.R. 1984: Head of department or learning advisor? *Remedial Education*, 19(2).

Clunies-Ross, L.R. 1984: Supporting the mainstream teacher. *Special Education*, 11(3).

Coffield, F., Robinson, P. and Sarsby, J. 1980: *A Cycle of Deprivation?* Heinemann.

Cohn, R. 1969: The Theme-centred Interactional Method. *Journal of Group Psychoanalysis and Process*, 2(2).

Collins, M. 1969: *Students into Teachers.* Routledge and Kegan Paul.

Conoley, J.C. (ed.). 1981: *Consultation in Schools.* Academic Press.

Cope, E. 1971: *School Experience in Teacher Education* (Vol. I), *A Study of a School-Supervised Practice* (Vol. II). University of Bristol School of Education.

Crompton, M. 1980: *Respecting Children.* Arnold.

Cropper, L. 1980: Children and stories. *Forum for the Advancement of Educational Therapy, Newsletter 7.*

Daines, R. *et al.* 1981: *Child Guidance and Schools — A Study of a Consultation Service.* Department of Social Work, School of Applied Social Studies, University of Bristol.

Dainton, F.S. (chairman) 1968: *Enquiry into the Flow of Candidates in Science and Technology into Higher Education*. HMSO.

Davies, G. 1983: *Practical Primary Drama*. Heinemann.

De Cecco, J.P. and Schaeffer, G.A. 1978: Using negotiation to resolve teacher–student conflicts. *Journal of Research and Development in Education*, 11(4).

Delamont, S. 1976: *Interaction in the Classroom*. Methuen.

Department of Education and Science (DES), 1978: *Making INSET Work*. HMSO.

Department of Education and Science (DES), 1984: *Education Observed*. DES.

DES/DHSS Joint Circular 3/74/HSC(IS) 1974: *Child Guidance*. HMSO.

Dockar-Drysdale, B. 1973: *Consultation in Child Care*. Longman.

Dowling, E. 1985: Theoretical framework — a joint systems approach to educational problems with children. In Dowling, E. and Osborne, E. (eds.), *The Family and the School, A Joint Systems Approach to Problems with Children*. Routledge and Kegan Paul.

Dowling, E. and Osborne, E. (eds.), *The Family and the School, A Joint System Approach to Problems with Children*. Routledge and Kegan Paul.

Duffy, M. 1984: A view from the bridge. *Secondary Headteachers Association Discussion Document*.

Dunkley, S. 1980: Counselling in Mayfield School. *New Era*, 61(5).

Eavis, P. 1983: Expertise (review of *Becoming Our Own Experts*). *TES*, May 27.

Eggleston, J. 1977: *The Ecology of the School*. Methuen.

Elliott, J. 1982: The idea of a pastoral curriculum: a reply to T. H. McLaughlin. *Cambridge Journal of Education*, 12(1).

Ellis, S. 1985: The work of the DO5 schools support team. *Maladjustment and Therapeutic Education*, 3(2).

English, M. 1984: *Fans*. Cambridge University Press.

Eraut, M. 1977: Strategies for promoting teacher development. *British Journal of In-Service Education*, 4(1, 2).

Eraut, M. 1977: Some perspective on consultancy in in-service education. *British Journal of In-Service Education*, 4(1, 2).

Erikson, E.H. 1980: *Identity and the Life Cycle*. Norton.

Ferri, E. 1984: *Stepchildren*. NFER–Nelson.

Fielker, L. 1980: The use of literature to encourage an understanding of the emotions: a record of work with disturbed adolescents. *MA (Ed.) Thesis*, (unpublished) Goldsmiths College.

Fitzherbert, K. 1977: *Childcare Services and the Teacher*. Temple Smith.

Flanders, N. 1970: *Analysing Teaching Behaviour*. Addison-Wesley.

Foulkes, S.H. and Anthony, E.J. 1965: *Group Psychotherapy*. Penguin (2nd edn.).

Fuller, A. 1980: Counselling in schools in 1980. *New Era*, 61(5).

Fulton, J.F. 1980: Guidance and counselling in schools. *New Era*, 61(5).

Galloway, D. 1985: *Schools, Pupils and Special Educational Needs*. Croom Helm.

Galloway, D.M. and Goodwin, C. 1979: *Educating Slow-learning and Maladjusted Children: Integration or Segregation?* Longman.

Garrett, J. 1983: Presidential address. *National Council for Special Education Newsletter 11*(2).

Gillham, B. (ed.) 1978: *Reconstructing Educational Psychology*. Croom Helm.

Gipps, C. 1982: Nursery nurses and nursery teachers. *Journal of Child Psychology and Psychiatry*, 23(3).

Gipps, C. and Goldstein, H. 1984: More than a change in name? *Special Education*, 11(4).

Gliedman, J. and Roth, W. 1981: Parents and professionals. In *The Practice of Special Education*. Open University.

Goldacre, P. 1980: Helping children with bereavement. *Therapeutic Education*, 8(2).

Goldacre, P. 1985: Working with bereaved children. *Journal of Educational Therapy*, to be published.

Gosling, R. 1965: *The Use of Small Groups in Training*. Codicote Press.

Graham, D. 1984: Will teacher assessment ever get off the ground? *TES*, November 23.

Gulliford, R. 1971: *Special Educational Needs*. Routledge and Kegan Paul.

Gulliford, R. 1975: Enrichment methods. In Wedell, K. (ed.), *Orientations in Special Education*. Wiley.

Hamblin, D.H. 1975: The counsellor and strategies for the treatment of disturbed children in the secondary school. *British Journal of Guidance and Counselling*, 3(2).

Hamblin, D.H. 1978: *The Teacher and Pastoral Care*. Basil Blackwell.

Hanko, G. 1982: *An Account and Evaluation of the Development of School-based Consultancy Support and Training Groups for Teachers of Disturbed and Disturbing Children in Ordinary Schools*. University of London Institute of Education, unpublished report.

Hannam, C., Smyth, P. and Stephenson, N. 1976: *The First Year of Teaching*. Penguin.

Hargreaves, D.H. 1967: *Social Relations in a Secondary School*. Routledge and Kegan Paul.

Hargreaves, D.H. 1972: *Interpersonal Relations and Education*. Routledge and Kegan Paul.

Harris, P.L., Olthof, T. and Terwogt, M.M. 1981: Children's knowledge of emotion. *Journal of Child Psychology and Psychiatry*, 22(3).

Heathcote, D. and Wagner, B.J. 1979: *Drama as a Learning Medium*. Hutchinsons.

Hegarty, S. and Pocklington, K. 1981: *Educating Pupils with Special Needs in the Ordinary School*. NFER–Nelson.

Hider, A.T. 1981: *The Schools and In-Service Teacher Education (SITE) Evaluation Project in Ealing 1978–1980*. University of Bristol School of Education Research Unit.

Hill, J. 1975: The transition from school to work. *Secondary Education*, 5(1).

Hodgkinson, P.E. 1985: Staff support systems in the residential treatment of adolescents. *Maladjustment and Therapeutic Education*, 3(1).

Hornby, S. 1983: Collaboration in social work. *Journal of Social Work Practice*, 1(1).

Hughes, M., Mayall, B., Moss, P., Perry, J., Petrie, P. and Pinkerton, G. 1980: *Nurseries Now*. Penguin.

Irvine, E.E. 1959: The use of small group discussions in the teaching of human relations and mental health. *British Journal of Psychiatric Social Work*, 6.

Irvine, E.E. 1979: *Social Work and Human Problems: Casework, Consultation and Other Topics*. Pergamon.

James, C. 1980: *Unreliable Memoirs*. Picador.

Johnson, L. and O'Neill, C. (eds.) 1984: *Dorothy Heathcote, Collected Writings on Education and Drama*. Hutchinson.

Jones, A. 1980: The school's view of persistent non-attendance. In Hersov and Berg (eds.), *Out of School*. Wiley.

Jones, A. 1985: Pastoral care and community education. *Pastoral Care in Education*, 3(2).

Jones, R.M. 1968: *Fantasy and Feeling in Education*. ULP and Penguin.

Kadushin, A. 1977: *Consultation in Social Work*. Columbia University Press, NY.

Kahn, J. 1974: Institutional constraints to interprofessional practice.

In Rehr, H. (ed.), *Medicine and Social Work: An Exploration in Interprofessionalism*. Prodist, NY.

Kahn, J. and Wright, S.E. 1980: *Human Growth and the Development of Personality*. Pergamon (3rd edn.).

Karpf, A. 1985: Boys won't always be boys. *Guardian*, March 12.

Knight, J. 1982: Making connections. *TES*, May 7.

Kolvin, I., Garside, R.E., Nicol, A.R., Macmillan, A., Wolstenholme, E. and Leitch, I.M. 1982: *Help Starts Here*. Tavistock.

Kounin, J.S., Friesen, W.V. and Norton, A.E. 1965: Managing emotionally disturbed children in regular classrooms. *Journal of Educational Psychology*, 57(1).

Lacey, C. 1977: *The Socialization of Teachers*. Methuen.

Lang, P. 1983: How pupils see it: looking at how pupils perceive pastoral care. *Pastoral Care in Education*, 1(3).

Laslett, R. 1977: *Educating Maladjusted Children*. Crosby Lockwood Staples.

Laslett, R. 1982: Maladjusted children in the ordinary school. *National Council for Special Education, Developing Horizons Series*, 3.

Laslett, R. and Smith, C. 1984: *Effective Classroom Management: A Teacher's Guide*. Croom Helm.

Lewis, G. 1984: A supportive role at secondary level. *Remedial Education*, 19(1).

Lewis, M.M. 1963: *Language, Thought and Personality in Infancy and Childhood*. Harrap.

Lim, M.H. and Bottomley, V. 1983: A combined approach to the treatment of effeminate behaviour in a boy. *Journal of Child Psychology and Psychiatry*, 24(3).

Lindsey, C. 1985: Some aspects of consultation to primary schools. In Dowling, E. and Osborne, E. (eds.), *The Family and the School, A Joint Systems Approach to Problems with Children*. Routledge and Kegan Paul.

Livingstone, C. 1984: *Role Play in Language Learning*. Longman.

Longley, J. 1980: Counselling in a girls' school. *New Era*, 61(5).

Lyons, K.H. 1973: *Social Work and the School: Aspects of the Role of an Education Social Worker*. HMSO.

Madge, N. 1983: Unemployment and its effects on children. *Journal of Child Psychology and Psychiatry*, 24(2).

Maher, P. 1985: The frontiers of teacher responsibility. *Pastoral Care in Education*, 3(1).

Marland, M. 1980: The pastoral curriculum. In Best, R., Jarvis, C. and Ribbins, P. (eds.), *Perspectives in Pastoral Care*. Heinemann.

Marland, M. 1984: The why and how of racism. *TES*, September 14.

Martin, N., Williams, P., Wilding, J., Hemmings, S. and Medway, P. 1976: *Understanding Children Talking*. Penguin.

Mayes, M. 1985: Some thoughts on allocating form tutors. *Pastoral Care in Education*, 3(1).

McLaughlin, T.H. 1982: The idea of a pastoral curriculum. *Cambridge Journal of Education*, 12(1).

McMahon, A., Bolam, R., Abbott, R. and Holly, P. 1984: Guidelines for review and internal development in schools. *Schools Council Programme 1, Purpose and Planning in Schools*. Longman.

Mearns, C. and Kay, B. 1985: Referred but not seen. *Association for Child Psychology and Psychiatry*, Newsletter, 7(3).

Medway, P. 1976: Back with Nellie. *British Journal of Teacher Education*, 2(2).

Meier, W. 1979: Meeting special needs through movement and dance drama. *Therapeutic Education*, 7(1).

Meltzer, D. 1979: The parents and educational conflict. *Discussion Paper, Forum for the Advancement of Educational Therapy*.

Milgram, S. 1974: *Obedience to Authority*. Tavistock.

Mitchell, P. 1985: The quality controllers. *Bedford Way Papers*, 22. Heinemann.

Mittler, P. 1983: The challenge of teacher training: doing more and more with less and less. *Secondary Education Journal*, 13(2).

Mittler, P. 1984: *New Frontiers*. Northampton Conference Report, National Council for Special Education.

Mittler, P. 1985: British Psychological Society Conference Report. *TES*, January 18.

Mittler, P. and Mittler, H. 1982: Partnership with parents. *National Council for Special Education, Developing Horizons Series 2*.

Montgomery, D. 1984: *Learning Difficulties Project: Evaluation and Enhancement of Teaching Performance, A Pilot Study*. Kingston Polytechnic.

Morris, B. 1965: How does a group learn to work together? In Niblett, W.R. (ed.), *How and Why do we Learn?* Faber and Faber.

Morris, B. 1972: *Objectives and Perspectives in Education*. Routledge and Kegan Paul.

Muncey, J. and Ainscow, M. 1983: Launching SNAP in Coventry. *Special Education*, 10(3).

Musgrave, P.W. 1979: *The Sociology of Education*. Methuen (3rd edn.).

Nash, R. 1976: *Teacher Expectations and Pupil Learning*. Routledge and Kegan Paul.

National Association for Remedial Education (NARE) 1979: *NARE Guidelines No. 2, The Role of Remedial Teachers*.

National Association for Remedial Education (NARE) 1982: *NARE Guidelines No. 4, In-service Education for Remedial Teachers*.

Oakeshott, E. 1973a: *The Child under Stress*. Priory.

Oakeshott, E. 1973b: Defining educational therapy. *Inaugural Lecture, Forum for the Advancement of Educational Therapy*.

Osborne, E. 1985: The teachers' view: working with teachers out of the school setting. In Dowling, E. and Osborne, E. (eds.), *The Family and the School*. Routledge and Kegan Paul.

Paneth, E. 1980: *Tapes of your own*. Longman.

Pelleschi, A. 1985: Pastoral care and girls of Asian parentage. *Pastoral Care In Education*, 3(2).

Peters, R.S. 1974: *Psychology and Ethical Development*. Unwin.

Pinkus, L. and Dare, C. 1978: *Secrets in the Family*. Tavistock.

Plog, S.C. and Ahmed, P.I. 1977: *Principles and Techniques of Mental Health Consultation*. Plenum.

Porter, L.G. 1984: *Speaking Personally*. Cambridge University Press.

Posell, E. 1984: *Homecoming*. Heinemann.

Pugh, G. and De'Ath, E. 1984: *The Needs of Parents*. Macmillan.

Quicke, J. 1985: Charting a course for personal and social education. *Pastoral Care in Education*, 3(2).

Quinton, D. and Rutter, M. 1983: Parenting behaviour of mothers raised 'in care'. In Nicol, A.R. (ed.), *Practical Lessons for Longitudinal Studies*. Wiley.

Quinton, D. and Rutter, M. 1984: Parents with children in care. I: Current circumstances and parenting. II: Intergenerational continuities. *Journal of Child Psychology and Psychiatry*, 25(2).

Raven, J. 1977/78: School rejection and its amelioration. *Educational Research*, 20(1).

Redl, F. 1966: *When We Deal with Children*. New York Free Press.

Redl, F. and Winemann, D. 1957: *I, Children Who Hate. II, Controls from Within*. New York Free Press.

Redmond, M. 1975: Practice dignified. *University of London Institute of Education, Newsletter 6*.

Reik, T. 1947: *Listening with the Third Ear*. Allen and Unwin.

Ribbins, P. 1984: Review of Barnes, D. *Practical Curriculum Study. Pastoral Care in Education*, 2(2).

Ribbins, P. 1985: Pastoral care for children: welfare for teachers. In Ribbins, P. (ed.), *Schooling and Welfare*. Falmer.

Rice, A.K. 1971: *Learning for Leadership: Interpersonal and Intergroup Relations*. Tavistock.

Richardson, J.E. 1967: *Group Study for Teachers*. Routledge and Kegan Paul.

Richardson, J.E. 1973: *The Teacher, the School and the Task of Management*. Routledge and Kegan Paul.

Ridgway, B. 1984: Science games (review of *Science for Children with Learning Difficulties*. Macdonald Educational Learning through Science). *TES*, March 9.

Rowan, P. 1982: Social consequences. *TES*, November 12.

Rudduck, J. 1981: Making the most of the short in-service course. *Schools Council Working Paper 71*. Methuen.

Rutter, M. 1975: *Helping Troubled Children*. Penguin.

Rutter M. 1981: Stress, coping and development. *Journal of Child Psychology and Psychiatry*, 22(4).

Rutter, M. 1985: Family and school influences on behavioural development. *Journal of Child Psychology and Psychiatry*, 26(3).

Rutter, M., Maugham, B., Mortimore, P., Ouston, J. with Smith, A. 1979: *Fifteen Thousand Hours*. Open Books.

Salmon, P. (ed.) 1980: *Coming to Know*. Routledge and Kegan Paul.

Salzberger-Wittenberg, I., Henry, G. and Osborne, E. 1983: *The Emotional Experience of Learning and Teaching*. RKP.

Sayer, J. 1987: *Secondary Education for All?* Cassell.

Scharff, and Hill, J. 1976: *Between Two Worlds*. Careers Consultants.

Schein, E.H. 1969: *Process Consultation: Its Role in Organizational Development*. Addison-Wesley.

Schools Council, 1968: *Enquiry I, Young School Leavers*. HMSO.

Sewell, G. 1982: *Reshaping Remedial Education*. Croom Helm.

Shipman, M.D., Bolam, R. and Jenkins, D.R. 1974: *Inside a Curriculum Project*.

Sisterton, D. 1980: Counselling in the primary school. *New Era*, 61(5).

Skynner, A.C.R. 1974: An experiment in group consultation with the staff of a comprehensive school. *Group Process*, 6.

Smith, C.J. 1982: Helping colleagues cope — a consultant role for the remedial teacher. *Remedial Education*, 17(2).

Spencer, D. 1983: Report on Schools Council Conference. *TES*, June 3.

Stagles, B. 1985: What teachers like about active tutorial work. *Pastoral Care in Education*, 3(1).

Staines, J.W. 1971: The self-picture as a factor in the classroom. In *Personality Growth and Learning*. Open University/Longman.

Stott, D.H. 1982: Helping the maladjusted child. *Children with Special Needs Series*. Open University Press.

Summerfield Report 1968: *Psychologists in Education Services*. HMSO.

Sutherland, J.D. 1964: An additional role for the psychological clinic. In Balint, M (ed.), *The Doctor, His Patient and the Illness*. Pitman Medical (2nd edn.).

Tall, G. 1985: An evaluation of the introduction of Active Tutorial Work in a Birmingham comprehensive school. *Pastoral Care in Education*, 3(1).

Taylor, D. 1982: Family consultation in a school setting. *Journal of Adolescence*, 5(4).

Taylor, D. 1984: The child as go-between: consulting with parents and teachers. Paper delivered at the Nov. 1984 *Forum for the Advancement of Educational Therapy*.

Taylor, P. 1984: Pastoral care and in-service training, *Pastoral Care in Education*, 2(3).

Taylor, W. 1965: Learning to live with neighbours. In Niblett, W.R. (ed.), *How and Why do We Learn?* Faber and Faber.

Thacker, J. 1985: Extending developmental group work to junior/middle schools. *Pastoral Care in Education*, 3(1).

Tizard, B and Hughes, M. 1984: Young Children Learning. Fontana.

Tizard, J. 1973: Maladjusted children and the child guidance service. *London Educational Review*, 2(2).

Upton, G. 1983: Staff support systems. In Upton, G. (ed.), *Educating Children with Behaviour Problems*. Faculty of Education, University College, Cardiff.

Upward, R. 1984: *Wessex Studies in Special Education*. King Alfred's College, Winchester.

Visser, J. 1983: Special provision in the secondary school. In Upton, G. *Educating Children with Behaviour Problems*. Faculty of Education, University College, Cardiff.

Walker, E. 1981: Emotional recognition in disturbed and normal children. *Journal of Child Psychology and Psychiatry*, 22(3).

Wall, W.D. 1973: The problem child in schools. *London Educational Review*, 2(2).

Wall, W.D. 1977: *Constructive Education for Adolescents*. Harrap/ UNESCO.

Wall, W.D. 1979: *Constructive Education for Special Groups*. Harrap/ UNESCO.

Warnock, M. (chairman) 1978: *Special Educational Needs*. HMSO.

Warnock, M. 1982: Personal column, *TES*, October 1.

Welton, J. 1983: Pastoral care in the social division of welfare. *Pastoral Care in Education*, 1(2).

Werner, T. 1984: *Child Studies: Child Care and Development — A Two Year Course*. Batsford.

Wheldall, K. 1982: The behavioural approach to teaching (BAT project). *Association for Child Psychology and Psychiatry, News No. 13*.

Whiteside, T. 1978: *The Sociology of Educational Innovation*. Methuen.

Wilce, H. 1984: Walking the tight-rope between two cultures. *TES*, February 10.

Williamson, D. 1980: Pastoral care or 'pastoralization'. In Best, R., Jarvis, C. and Ribbins, P. (eds.) *Perspectives in Pastoral Care*. Heinemann.

Wilson, J. and Cowell, B. 1984: 'Pastoral care': some prevailing fantasies. *Pastoral Care in Education*, 2(2).

Wilson, M.D. 1981: *The Curriculum in Special Schools*. Schools Council/Methuen.

Wilson, M.D. 1983a: *Stories for Disturbed Children*. National Council for Special Education.

Wilson, M.D. 1983b: The curriculum for special needs. *Secondary Education Journal*, 13(2).

Wilson, M.D. and Evans, M. 1980: *The Education of Disturbed Pupils. Schools Council Working Paper 65*. Methuen.

Winnicott, D.W. 1965: *The Maturational Processes and the Facilitating Environment*. Hogarth.

Wolfendale, S. 1983: *Parental Participation in Children's Development and Education*. Gordon and Breach.

Wolff, S. 1969: *Children under Stress*. Allen Lane.

Wolff, S. 1983: Critical notice on Kolvin, I. *et al. Help Starts Here. Journal of Child Psychology and Psychiatry*, 24(4).

Wood, H.A. and Wood, D.J. 1984: An experimental evaluation of the effects of five styles of teacher conversation on the language of hearing-impaired children. *Journal of Child Psychology and Psychiatry*, 25(1).

Yule, W. 1974: Behavioural therapy. In Varma, V. (ed.), *Psychotherapy Today*. Constable.